CONVERSATION ABOUT AMERICA

The Faux-G.O.P.'s War against Right, Wrong, and Democracy

Thomas I. White

Desiderius Press

Library of Congress Control Number: 2017951795

ISBN 978-0-9837080-3-2

Desiderius Press

Table of Contents

CHAPTER ONE

The majestic sight of the lighted dome of the Capitol in the distance was thrilling. I hadn't felt this energized in years. We'd pulled off the trifecta: The White House, Senate and House! Years of fighting not only with the Democrats, but with people in my own party were finally behind me. Despite a rough start, I felt confident we were going to be able to come together and do something important for the country.

Standing in front of the elevator in the Rayburn Building, I was so impatient to get to my office and focus on business, I pushed the button repeatedly for the next 30 seconds.

"Practicing your Morse code?"

I turned to my right to see a tall, distinguished-looking gentleman. He was politely trying to hide that he'd been laughing at my impatience. The door slid open.

The two of us stepped in and moved to opposite sides of the car. I hit the button to my floor. When nothing happened, I punched it a few times more.

The stranger chuckled again as the doors closed.

I forced a polite smile. Impatience is a weakness I'm working on. I was embarrassed that the first impression I'd made was negative. I learned early on in D.C. that you never know who strangers may turn out to be.

I tried to see what I could conclude about my elevator mate. Tall, mid-50s, salt and pepper hair, athletic, with one of those odd beards that goes along the chin line. No briefcase. Just a thin tablet. The more important you are in this town, the less you carry. That's what your minions are for.

Some sort of heavy hitter? His clothes gave that impression. He wore an expensive charcoal, three-piece suit. His tie surprised me. It was a conservative regimental stripe, but the dominant color was bright pink. So, he was traditional in some ways, bold in others. I knew he wasn't in Congress because I'd have recognized him. I couldn't see a visitor's ID badge, but he may have stuffed it in his pocket. A lobbyist? A donor? He looked vaguely familiar.

"Excuse me. Have we met?"

He glanced over and simply shook his head 'no.'

"Are you sure? The more I think of it, I could swear we've crossed paths." Then it hit me. "You know, you bear a striking resemblance to—"

He laughed. "I get that all the time. It must be the beard. I can assure you, Congressman, we've never met. However, I do know who you are, and I was actually on looking to support a core group of men and women who will be tireless in reaffirming a commitment to ethics, democracy, and retaking America."

I was stunned by his diatribe. Revolution? Hatred of America? Undermining democracy? Minority rule? I hoped he was exaggerating and just being dramatic, but he looked serious. If he was looking for a firebrand radical like himself, that wasn't me.

Still, while I hated to admit it, parts of his tirade resonated with me. I wasn't comfortable with how strident and uncompromising my more conservative colleagues typically were. I certainly couldn't support their attitude that 'we're right, everyone else is wrong, and we'll do whatever we can to advance our agenda until someone stops us.' I'd stopped counting the number of actions, policies, or comments that revealed their shameless lack of compassion. I was genuinely heartsick that the White House was now a symbol of moral blindness. And I was *deeply* troubled by the combination of an assault on the FBI, the DOJ, and the intelligence community and a refusal to punish Russia for their attack on our election.

I'd love to be able to improve things in D.C. But was there a match here? I didn't know.

My companion was waiting for a response. As I brooded, he frowned. Then he crossed his arms and said seriously, "I'm not going to lie. Your lack of enthusiasm suggests there's no fit. I can see the wheels turning in your head. You're doing your normal calculations. You've apparently become one of those politicians who's more concerned with staying in the good graces of the radicals running your party and getting re-elected than actually doing something positive. When I told our group I wanted to talk to you, one of my colleagues said not to bother. 'He's been in politics too long,' she said. 'He's forgotten everything that made him a great CEO. He can't get it back.' I disagreed, and I also don't like to make hasty decisions."

I wasn't happy he was dismissing me so quickly—or that he'd basically read my mind. "Calculations like that are part of the game. You know that. So I'm not going to apologize. But since we're both in the dark about each other, I have a suggestion. Let's go one step at a time, and we'll see what we can find out." I had no idea whether I could work with him, but I wanted more time to evaluate the possibility. If nothing else, he and I were alike in wanting our decisions to be careful and well-informed.

He nodded agreement.

"We'll start with a few questions about some basic principles to make sure we're at least in the same ballpark. If you're truly the 'traditional, mainstream Republican' you claim to be, you shouldn't have any trouble with them. If we have agreement there, we'll move on to our discussion of specific values."

That seemed like a sensible approach. I nodded.

"These are important and might get complicated, so think before you answer."

I leaned in to show I was listening carefully. "OK."

"First, it is wrong to yell 'Fire' in a crowded theatre when there's no danger?"

I leaned back, furrowed my brow, and looked at him skeptically. Complicated? Is he for real?

"You're serious? This is how we start a discussion about the fundamental values on which the country is based?"

He frowned. "Is there a problem? Is this too tough?"

I let out a laugh. The way his face turned dour said he didn't appreciate my response, but I couldn't help myself. "OK. I'll play. Of course it's wrong! It's so obvious, it's crazy you'd imagine anyone would think otherwise."

He paused and looked at me. "You think it's *that* obvious? We'll see. ... Now tell me *why* it's wrong."

"You mean it's not *obvious*? You really have to ask?"

"Humor me," he smiled.

"OK. It's wrong because innocent people will get hurt!"

"How?" He responded seriously.

"What do you mean? As I said, all this is obvious!"

"Maybe so. But," he glanced at the closed doors, "it's

not like we're going anywhere soon. I'm genuinely curious about *exactly* what you think makes it wrong when someone yells 'Fire!' in that situation."

His expression said he expected a detailed answer. Since I wasn't going anywhere, there was no harm in accommodating him. I thought for a moment. "The warning makes people think there's danger when there isn't any. Their fear then makes them do something they assume will save them. But it actually gets them hurt."

He relaxed at the fact that I finally took his request seriously. "And the person who yells fire is *responsible* for that?"

"Yes, he or she is responsible for the harm."

He nodded approvingly.

"Question two. Is it wrong *not* to warn people when there actually is a fire in the theatre?"

I paused. "Interesting. Covering every angle? Yes. That's wrong too. If you don't warn everyone, people will get hurt. Of course, you want to do this in a way that doesn't cause a panic and produce even more harm. But failing to warn people is wrong."

"Good. So, it can be wrong to *do nothing* when someone might get hurt? In certain situations, we can be *responsible for harm* when we *don't* do something?"

I hesitated. The look in his eyes told me I'd underestimated him. There was a strategy behind these

14

apparently simple-minded questions. I had the feeling I was being set up. But I was curious to see how this would play out.

"Yes. Common sense says the right thing to do is warn people when you can prevent them from getting hurt."

He nodded again, then pointed at my watch. "That's an unusual timepiece for a Member of Congress."

I held out my arm so he could get a better look. It was a Mickey Mouse watch. "My wife got it for me when I won my first election. She said it should always remind me my job was to look out for everyone's children. I prize this more than anything else I own."

He smiled. "Smart woman. May I look at it?"

I hesitated.

"Don't worry. I promise to return it. Scout's honor." He smiled and held up two fingers.

I realized I was being silly and handed it to him. He studied it, then slid it in his pocket.

"OK. Moving on. Imagine you're having dinner at home with your family. It's time for dessert."

I frowned. "Wait a minute. I'd like my watch back first."

He stared back blankly. "Why?"

"Because it's mine, and you promised to return it."

"Yes, I did. Didn't I? I didn't just *hint* I'd give it back. I explicitly said, 'I promise' and 'Scout's honor,' didn't I? But wait a minute. I wasn't a Scout. I lied. So, it didn't count. As I was saying, imagine you're having dinner—"

He was clearly up to something. "OK. What's this about?"

He smirked as he took my watch out of his pocket and held it up. "Let me understand this. You think that my saying 'I promise' meant I'd return it."

"Obviously."

"Promises are important to you."

"Yes."

He raised his eyebrows. "That's an odd attitude for a politician."

"Maybe for others. But I tell my constituents I won't make promises I can't keep. I disappoint a lot of potential voters during a campaign. But I learned in business that you're only as good as your word."

He smiled and handed my watch back to me. "I just wanted a closer look. Tell your wife how impressed I am with her idea of using it as a way to keep you on target. So, we agree it's important to keep promises?"

I nodded. *Note to self. Watch your step with this guy.*

"Back to dinner, then. It's time for dessert. There's plenty of fruit, but only one piece of cake. Everyone around the table is eyeing it. You suggest that in situations like this, the right thing to do is take turns choosing first.

You propose that today the order will be: the youngest, second youngest, your wife, and you. First pick will change each day. This arrangement works fine—until a week later when you realize you're going to get stuck with a dessert you can't stand. So, you say, 'I think it's always a good experience to mix things up. Let's start with the oldest now.' And guess who that is? You, of course. ... So, what do you think about what you did?"

I sighed that he was back to asking questions the answers to which were insultingly obvious. "It's transparently unfair, hypocritical, and self-serving. And," I smiled, "I'm breaking a promise." He smiled approvingly. "I'm not fooling anyone with my 'value of new experiences' nonsense. All I care about is getting what I want."

"Why hypocritical?" he asked.

"I like the rules when they get me what I want. I change them when they work against me."

"Excellent. Next, imagine you're discussing your tax return with your accountant. You tell her, 'When you're calculating what I *owe*, 'one plus one plus one plus one' will equal 'three.' When you're determining my *refund*, 'one plus one plus one plus one' will equal 'five.' Your opinion?"

I shook my head and laughed. "You know, you're officially *weird*."

He smiled. "So I'm told. You still need to answer my

question."

"You know as well as I do that adding four 'ones' can't equal anything but 'four.'"

"Really? Are you sure?" He gave me a thoroughly puzzled look. It was transparently disingenuous. "Can you show me?"

His smirk confirmed it. I was *definitely* being set up. I took four business cards out of my pocket. I placed one on the floor. "One." I put down a second. "Plus one." Then the third. "Plus one." "And the fourth. "Plus one." Then I pointed at them one at a time. "Equals one, two, three, *four.*"

He raised his eyebrows, furrowed his forehead and looked like he wasn't sure. "Hmmm. Does it work like that every time?"

I laughed. "Not only *every time*, it even works with different objects." I put down my phone—"One." My business card case—"Plus one." Then a pen—"Plus one"—and a pencil—"Plus one. Equals," Then I pointed at them one at a time, "One, two, three, *four.*"

"Remarkable! Even with different sorts of objects? Wow!" He tried to look awestruck.

"OK, smartass. Do you want to tell me what kind of game you're playing? If you wanted to talk about fundamental American values, why start with this stuff? In particular, what does arithmetic have to do with right and wrong?"

He just smiled. "Patience is a virtue—in life and in politics."

It was clear he wasn't going to tell me anything at this point.

"So, let's take stock of where we've arrived at so far. Is it fair to say that you agree with these principles? Ones that my group considers to be bedrock when it comes to traditional American values." He held up a finger as he ticked them off. "It's wrong to cause harm. It's wrong to fail to prevent harm. It's wrong to break promises. It's wrong to be unfair and hypocritical."

I waited. "What about 1+1+1+1?"

"Don't worry, we'll come back to that. So?"

"So?"

"Can I assume that you agree with these principles?"

"Of course, I do. Who wouldn't? You'd have to be a criminal or pond scum not to."

"You're sure? I don't you to complain about being trapped into saying something you don't truly believe?"

His face. His tone. Everything about him said, *smug*. I groaned. What's this guy playing at? I gave him the finger.

He laughed. "I suppose I deserved that. Glad to see some spine. We'll take that as a *yes*."

"If you're done playing games, can we just—"

"Final question. I promise," he interrupted. "How has

your *behavior* measured up against these principles? Ever yell 'Danger!' when there's been no threat?"

I looked at the door. Trapped with someone who's taken 'annoying' to an art form, I had no choice but to keep playing along.

"Absolutely not."

"Ever *not* yell 'Danger!' when you should have?"

"Of course not."

"Keep promises?"

"Yes."

"Changed the rules to get what you wanted?"

"Absolutely not. The rules are the rules."

"And did you ever play fast and loose with 1 + 1 +1 + 1?"

"Do I look that stupid?"

He struggled to suppress a grin. "No, you don't. But, of course, that's what I'm trying to find out. Isn't it?"

"OK. Enough with the insults. Why don't you j——"

He held up his hand.

"There will be plenty of time to get into the details. But first I want to thank you for being so cooperative about what surely felt like an obvious and insulting exercise." The smugness was gone, and he was addressing me with genuine respect and appreciation. "To be honest, what I was listening for wasn't *what* you said, but *how* you said it. In this town, everyone talks a great game. I needed to know you that you really meant what you said. And I'd know that only if we were face to face. I'd very much like to continue our conversation if you're still game."

I took a moment to decide what I'd learned about my companion so far. He was smart, clever, committed to his cause. And he could be *really* annoying—but in a way I found interesting. I was intrigued.

"Lay on, Macduff."

He stretched and winced in a way that suggested his back was sore.

"I guess this floor isn't as comfortable as I thought. And you look like you could use some exercise. Washington's a beautiful city. The weather is on our side. I say we start by going for a walk." He pulled out his phone, tapped out a text, and the doors popped open.

I did a double take. "Hey! I thought you said you didn't have a phone."

He just shrugged. "No, I said I didn't *believe* in them. I don't. But that doesn't mean I don't use one when I need to. Someone as slippery as you can be with language should appreciate the distinction. And call your office. Tell them to cancel your morning appointments because you're meeting with a possible donor. We're going to be awhile. We don't want your people to think you've been kidnapped."

He was up on his feet and headed out the building

with a speed that put me to shame. As I started to follow, the head of maintenance approached me and insisted on apologizing profusely. I had to scramble to catch my companion, and I was breathing hard when I pulled alongside. Seeing my difficulty, he slowed down. He couldn't resist, "Sound mind, sound body, Congressman."

We crossed a couple of streets and started walking along the Mall.

When we established a comfortable pace, he turned my way. "Let's get into specifics. Where do you stand on *respect*, Congressman?"

CHAPTER TWO

I was relieved we'd finally gotten to what we were supposed to be discussing. The 'shouting fire,' '*not* shouting fire,' 'promise,' 'cake' and '1 + 1 + 1 + 1' questions were easy enough to handle. But that's not the way I'd start a discussion about the country's values. Maybe he wanted to see if he could rattle me with something out of left field. No. That was too simple. He was too clever for that. I'd find out eventually. In the meantime, I was happy to plunge in.

"I believe that *respect* is part of the bedrock of America," I replied passionately. "It's important for us to respect the basic vision of the Founding Fathers as expressed in our Constitution. This means recognizing the primary role of the states and local government. Limiting the role of government in business and letting the market do its job. More broadly in society, this means honoring the traditions and customs that have been in place for a long time that give communities stability. And, of course, it's important to respect the police and military—the men and women who put their lives on the line every day to protect us."

Shaking his head, he shot me a grim glance. Looking away, he mumbled something I couldn't hear.

"You know, you have an odd way of showing approval. How can you *not* be happy with that answer? Was there anything wrong with what I said?"

He took a deep breath and sighed. "No, Congressman, you didn't say anything *wrong*. The problem is you didn't say *anything at all*. I told you I wanted to find out about your *core values*, not your political ideology. I thought you were listening when I said we believed that *right*, *wrong*, *honesty*, and *decency* were under assault. I thought you understood that when I said *respect*, it meant something about *ethics—moral* values—not *political positions* you'd tout to sell yourself to potential voters. He stared straight ahead silently for a few steps. "I'm sorry to have wasted your time. Apparently, I've made a mistake." He pulled out his phone.

I felt sandbagged. "Wait! Setting aside why you lied to me about that phone in the elevator, I think I deserve more of an explanation than just that you made a mistake. OK, I went down the wrong road. But I was trying to give you a serious answer about how important *respect* is to me. This is Washington, D.C. Remember? We're discussing whether your organization will support my next campaign. Why wouldn't I think you wanted a political answer?"

He stopped, looked down at me, and nodded. "You're right. I didn't give you any guidance about what we mean by 'fundamental American values.' But that was deliberate. As you pointed out, this is D.C.—where politicians are only too happy to tell anyone with money exactly what you think we want to hear. I'd hoped that if it was just the two of us, you'd have an easier time remembering your 'true self,' and—to use your image—you'd go down the right road of your own accord. If you felt that was unfair, I apologize. I suppose the decent thing for me to do is explain what I mean *this* time. When we get to the other values my group is concerned about, you'll have to find your own way—or not."

Despite the implied threat, there was nothing menacing about what he'd said. His people had a clear mission. They were looking for individuals who would champion those values on the Hill. I respected that. He was just stating a fact. However, his tone *did* communicate serious disappointment, so I was determined to get back in the game. But it wasn't just to line up a big donor. Despite the short amount of time we'd spend together, there was something about this man that I trusted. He was straightforward. He radiated intelligence, integrity, strength, and purpose. Those were the traits we always tried to hire for in my company. To be honest, I missed people like that—talented, 'no bullshit' individuals who were more concerned about solving problems than anything else. Also, I couldn't explain it, but I honestly felt that if we took enough time, we'd see we *agreed* about more than we *disagreed*. If I was wrong about this, fine. But I wanted our exchange to play itself out to a natural conclusion.

"I appreciate that," I said. "Trust me. You'll find me a quick study."

He chuckled as we started walking again. "Maybe too quick for your own good, Congressman."

I laughed as well. I knew that my ability to dance around a difficult question until I found something that worked as a neutral sound bite wasn't always a strength.

"So, here's how my associates and I view *respect*. Think about how America got established in the first place. We had a revolution against an authoritarian monarchy, and we opted for a democracy because we believe people deserve to be free and to make our own decisions about how we live. One of this country's key beliefs is that people shouldn't simply be told what to do. Everyone is entitled to have an equal hand in determining their fate. Moreover, in our system, *every citizen counts*—just by virtue of being a citizen. Nothing else matters—not family heritage, connections, class, wealth, or skin color. In our democracy, all citizens are equal and deserve the same respect.

"In a country that prizes individual freedom as strongly as we do, it's inevitable that people will have different goals. Americans think about lots of things differently. That means we need to manage this situation with civility. To accept each other as equal citizens. To respect the dignity of friend and adversary alike. All of us have to tolerate viewpoints very different from our own.

"Democracy is difficult enough even under the best conditions. But if we decide fellow citizens who disagree with us are our enemies, we can kiss democracy goodbye. After all, when we stop seeing people who have a different perspective from ours as equals who are entitled to be heard, we can rationalize treating them in whatever miserable way we want. It's always easier to kick people around whom we've already demonized.

"So that's what I mean by saying *respect* is a key value for America. It's a core ethical idea for us. Put it as simply as 'treating people as you'd want them to treat you,' if you want. It's not rocket science. It's basic decency."

As his explanation went on, he became more animated and passionate. Then he stopped walking, pointed his finger at me and punctuated every couple of words with a sharp jab.

"I can't think of anything more vital to the health of

American democracy than the kind of respect for each other I'm talking about. And looking at the other side of the coin," his expression went grim again, "I can't think of anything more fatal to American democracy than to decide that respect is a sign of weakness—a trait of losers and wimps."

"I couldn't agree more. Respect was a key value at my company as well."

"Great. We agree on the principle. But would you say your actions show a strong commitment to treating others with this kind of respect?"

"Without a doubt. Even in business, I was never one of those guys who thought you had to claw your way to the top over the bodies of friends and foes alike. I'm proud that, no matter whom I deal with, I try to treat them respectfully and to conduct our business with professionalism and courtesy."

I wasn't pleased that he cocked an eyebrow.

"OK, let's find out. Since we're talking about respect and civility, it just occurred to me that I never formally introduced myself. He extended his hand. "I'm Abe."

I had to laugh. With that beard, he was an amazing lookalike. As we shook, I replied in kind. "It's good to meet you, Abe. I'm Congressman Ste—."

He held up his hand to stop me talking. Then he leaned back as though he wanted to get a better look at me. "No, I don't think so."

"Excuse me?"

"I don't see you as a 'Congressman So-and-so.'" He crossed his arms, squinted, and studied me. "You look more like 'Dumb Ass.'" He virtually spat out the epithet as he waved his hand dismissively my way.

I didn't know whether I was more surprised by the incongruity of an insult following his impassioned defense of 'respect' or the fact that he went from polite and refined to being a jerk in a flash.

He looked puzzled. "You don't agree? I apologize. You're right. I got it wrong. 'Dumb Ass' has no rhythm. I think 'Shit for Brains Stephen' has a better cadence."

I ground my teeth. I didn't know what he was up to. It had to be some sort of test, but I didn't like games. I looked away, trying to decide how to respond.

"Pay attention, Bozo," he interrupted. "I know what name is on your office door. But we're operating under *new rules* about how we refer to each other now, aren't we? Like I know that you call your daughter in college 'Maureen.' But from what I hear, 'Popular Mo, the friendly ho' is a better fit." He added a lurid wink. "It looks like she's taking after her mother, '*Randy* Randy'? I've seen her picture. I bet it still applies. Lucky you." He let out a nasty laugh. "How did someone as ordinary as you land such a hottie? Talk about punching above your weight class!" The delight in his face said this wasn't an act and that he genuinely enjoyed taunting me and insulting my family.

My years in public life had required me to develop a tough skin when it came to insults directed at me. But I'd always felt that a politician's family was off limits. I was steaming inside, but I gritted my teeth and refused to take the bait. This jerk didn't know the first thing about 'respect.' I wouldn't take his campaign money if he was my only chance to win.

I shot him a steely look. "I don't know what you're playing at, but you can save yourself the trouble of deciding whether your group will back me. We see the world too differently for there to be a match. But *I'm* a gentleman. So let's shake hands and part company."

When I extended my hand, he let out a derisive laugh. "Ha! I guess I should have gone with 'Sissy Stevie the Ball-less Wonder! I insult your wife and daughter and the best you can do is, *'We see the world too differently for there to be a match?'*" A mean glint sparked in his eye. "You know, we haven't talked about your son George yet. The one with that birth defect? Don't you think 'Gimpy George' is more colorful and accurate? I bet the kids at school have a field day mocking him."

He began walking again. I stood still and glared at his back. When he turned to see where I'd gone, I pulled my phone out of my pocket and threw it at him as hard as I could. I was surprised he caught it so easily. He walked back to where I was standing. He scrunched up his face as though he was trying to understand some impossibly difficult concept.

"You're angry? I don't understand. Are you telling me you're uncomfortable with the *new rules* your guy has ushered in—rules that your party is happy to follow? How can that be? When you were that wunderkind CEO, you regularly talked about the 'tone from the top' when it came to setting the values for your company. Are you a hypocrite on top of everything else? You meant it then, but not now? Ha! Why would we even consider backing someone as wishy washy as you?"

I snatched my phone out of his hand and stuffed it back in my pocket. I was so angry I stood there clenching and unclenching my fists. I'd already lost my temper once. He wasn't going to make me do it again. As far as I was concerned, that was the end of our conversation.

Then his entire demeanor changed. The mean jerk was gone. His affect was back to that of a calm, distinguished gentleman. He put his hand on my shoulder.

"I have two questions for you, Congressman. First, what have we just learned?"

Damn! I should have known. I glared back. I was still furious. "Learned? Other than that you're either a low-life son-of-a-bitch who gets off on being nasty or has an easy time pretending to be one just to screw around with people?"

"Take a breath, Congressman, and let's keep walking," he smiled reassuringly. "That was a test having to do with respect. I'm happy to say that—unlike before—you passed this time. We reveal our values in our actions, not our words. You showed there was a limit to how much disrespect you'd tolerate—especially towards your family. Nice throw, by the way. But, again, what have we just learned?"

I forced myself to calm down. This guy knew how to push my buttons. I needed to be more careful. If we ended up too far apart to work together, I'd find myself in his crosshairs. I needed to stop revealing my weaknesses. If nothing else, I wanted to continue the conversation for my own protection. If we were going to be enemies, I wanted to understand how he operated.

I narrowed my eyes. "What have I learned? To be more suspicious of anyone with an uncanny resemblance to—"

He laughed. "Seriously. Put your CEO hat back on. What did our exchange just illustrate about disrespect and doing business?"

When I shifted perspectives, I knew exactly what he was thinking. "If we'd had this exchange when I was

CEO, as soon as you made your first crack, I would have ended the conversation. It wouldn't have been in a fit of pique or because you bruised my ego. It would have been because you'd revealed yourself as someone I couldn't trust.

"The CEO of some other company might have thought you were just sparring with them to see what they were made of. But in our company, respect and trust was a big deal. We saw ourselves as part of a team. We supported each other. A disrespectful and untrustworthy person wouldn't last long. And we wouldn't do business with someone like that, no matter how much money we could make. We've found that disrespect poisons relationships. Frankly, it makes a decent relationship impossible."

"Nicely put. See, when you stop thinking like a politician, it all comes back. ... Question two. When did you stop believing that?"

I did a double take. "*Stop?* Never. That's still what I believe."

"Really? That's not what your actions say."

I paused before answering. He was either trying to bait me again, or he was taking the long way around to make some kind of point.

"Why don't you save both of us some trouble and tell me what you're referring to?"

"The specifics? Your party—or at least the hijacked version of your party—gave us a Chief Executive who's a schoolyard bully and loves insulting people, right? And you all either look the other way or join in."

I shrugged. There was no way around it. "I don't approve, but that's just the way he is."

"I know how *he* is, Congressman. The question is how *you* are. Or, more precisely, how you *aren't*."

"You really like being oblique, don't you?" I quipped.

"More than you can *possibly* imagine," he said with a big smile. "But we agreed right off the bat that we can be responsible for *not* doing something. Correct?"

"Yes."

"So, what have you said or done in light of your guy's disrespectful behavior?"

"Well, like I said, that's just how he—"

He put his hand up. "Congressman, you aren't on the stump trying to walk some fine line to avoid offending a potential voter. It's just you and me, and we're going to be honest with each other. Let me save you some time. You did *nothing*. You remained silent while your Party's nominee trashed anyone who disagreed with him. Is that what you think acting like 'an American' means? Is that what the flag stands for to you? Behaving like an eight-year old brat in a schoolyard?"

He glanced towards the Washington Monument

which we were approaching. "Tell me, Congressman, in which of George Washington letters and speeches did he say that he fought to establish a country whose leaders get to piss on the citizens they're meant to serve?"

His face showed disgust.

"And not being content with insulting his countrymen, your guy decided to expand his reach—in a way that is truly unprecedented for an American president. *Shithole countries?* Tell me, Congressman. When was the last time your party gave us a president whose stupidity is exceeded only by his racism?" He threw his arms up in the air, and his face scrunched up as though he'd just tasted something vile.

"A handful of your colleagues strongly denounce all of this. But not you. The best you and most of your weak-willed cronies do is label things 'inappropriate.'

"What message do you suppose you send to the rest of the world? You already know the impact of the 'tone from the top.' If the chief honcho in an organization insults people, it becomes the norm. And that will make it impossible to do anything productive. You said it yourself. Disrespect poisons relationships—fatally."

He got inches from my face. "Or maybe it's worse than that you and your cronies are weak," he said calmly. "Maybe being a Republican means putting up with a racist bully so you can get something you want from him.

Is that it? Is going along with the idea that people deserve respect only if they're white your *price* for his signature on bills. Is that what you sold your virtue for? Which makes you—"

Despite the hard truth of what he was saying about my failure to do anything, it didn't feel like he was trying to beat me up. It was worse than that. He was calm and clinical. It was surgical. He was starting to fillet me. Now I saw why he began with the idea that we're responsible for the consequences of both what we *do* and *don't do*.

I hadn't been proud of my silence. When I was CEO, I never would have tolerated the sort of insulting and abusive behavior we saw daily. At my company, I wouldn't have thought twice before speaking out. If it continued, people would have been fired.

Abe was right. I'd stayed quiet hoping it was the best way to get elected and to operate in the current government.

"Times have changed. D.C. has changed. It's become a rougher place during my stint here. This is about being effective."

"Congressman," he sighed, "I am not a constituent you're trying to buffalo. I am someone who will be your friend—or your enemy. And I'm saying not so subtly that this is another time you failed to show any moral spine when it comes to respect."

"Another time?"

"Right. Don't tell me you've forgotten not treating President Obama with appropriate respect?"

"Obama? Are you kidding? I may not have been a big fan, but I never talked about him the way lots of my colleagues did—like he was the Devil incarnate. Besides, I shook his hand no more than three times. There have been precious few times I even had the opportunity to be disrespectful."

He nodded as though he was conceding my point and admitting he was wrong. "You're right. I owe you either an apology or an explanation."

I was surprised at how quickly he acknowledged his mistake. I relaxed.

"So, here's the *explanation* for why you should feel deeply ashamed—*again*—about how you failed to act."

I winced. I should have known he was going to do that.

"The way your guy started getting people's attention was to claim that President Obama wasn't really an American and, therefore, wasn't legitimately the President. You aren't going to pretend that racist nonsense about the birth certificate didn't happen, are you? The ongoing disgusting intimations that Obama was a Muslim, born in Africa, and that the birth certificate was a fake."

I brushed my hand through the air. "That was just a

sideshow. Whenever the press asked me about it, I told them to move on to something worthwhile. I couldn't believe anyone would take this stuff seriously. It was stupid. Why would they?"

"Stupid? Yes. And mean and disrespectful and racist. So, let's be clear about what was wrong with your not aggressively speaking out about this. We're still working with the idea that *doing nothing* can be as wrong as *doing something*, right?"

"True."

"OK, if 'silence means consent,' what did your silence about the birth certificate nonsense consent to?"

I had no desire to be tarred by something I thought was ridiculous from the start. I'd wait him out.

"No response? Suck it up, Congressman. What's the matter? Do the words taste so bad you can't even say them?"

He wasn't going to let me dodge this. "OK. Maybe some people would conclude that our silence meant we didn't mind such an offensive idea being put out there. The controversy made it more palatable to some people to object to Obama's policies."

He sighed. "That's an awfully sanitized way of putting it. Come on. Man up! What was the vile message that you and your Republican colleagues broadcast by not denouncing it?"

"If you're labeling it *vile*, I have a feeling that no matter how I put it, you'll keep asking for something else."

"You're right. You see yourself so much as a decent person I'm sure you still can't believe what your silence let spread out there. So here it is. The central message of the birther controversy was this: 'No *nigger* ever deserves to be President. If one got elec—"

"*NO!*" I shouted. I was shocked he'd suggest that's what we were really saying. "I would never say *anything* like that. And no one would have heard *that* as the message just because Republicans didn't object strongly enough to the birther nonsense. We're the Party of Lincoln, remember?"

Glaring at me, he just picked up where he left off. "'*If* one got elected, we get to do anything to throw him out.'

"I'm sorry to have to put this in such a crude and offensive way, Congressman, but this is too serious a matter to sugarcoat. Like it or not, whether you intended it or not, *that* was the message your silence conveyed. And you've only continued sending that message by conveniently ignoring the fact that your guy basically demonizes everyone who isn't white! All the racists in the country know that 'Make America Great Again' means 'Make America *White* Again.' Why don't you?"

The steely look said I should brace myself for more. He pointed at the Lincoln Memorial, now visible at the far end of the reflecting pool. "You're going to tell me within view of *that*, that you're the 'Party of Lincoln'? Did I get the Gettysburg Address wrong? I thought it said that our nation was 'dedicated to the proposition that all men are created equal.' I guess I forgot the part that says, 'unless you're the first Black President.' 'Party of Lincoln,' my ass! The G.O.P. has been the 'white people's' party for years. The fact that the Klan celebrated your guy getting elected should tell you something.

"And it's not just the birther garbage that sent that message. Every time leaders of your Party announced that you'd object to *whatever* President Obama put forward, you said it again: 'That *nigger* doesn't belong in the White House. We'll put that boy in his place.'" Like before, he jabbed his finger at me with each word—only this time with more anger.

"No! What we mea—"

"It doesn't matter what you tell yourself you meant, Congressman. The rest of America knew exactly what you were saying. Like it or not, the deliberate racism of the people who drove this has stuck onto you like tar because you stand too close to them.

"Barack Obama was the first African-American President. And he's the first President that *any* party ever treated this way in my lifetime. Are you telling me it was a *coincidence* that the only President who got treated this way is Black?

"That nonsense about not holding hearings on the President's Supreme Court nomination? Since 1912, six justices were confirmed during election years. Despite the normal posturing on both sides of the aisle about this in the past, no one ever pulled the trigger. And not only did your party go ahead and do it, you basically gave Obama the finger. You couldn't just hold hearings and vote down his nominee. No. You had to make up some new rule that applied only to our first African-American President even though a majority of the population thought Garland should be confirmed.

"Do you really think the American people are so stupid not to know what it means when the Faux-G.O.P.—the 'white people's party'—takes such a historic step? Do you expect me to believe you would have done that to a *white* President? Do you think it's an accident that racist incidents and hate crimes have increased since your guy got elected?

"And before you try to side-step this by limiting your Party's mistakes just to how you treated President Obama, remember your track record over the last couple of decades—gerrymandering voting districts to make them as pale as possible, and cutting back early voting wherever Black people would take advantage of it.

"You don't honestly think anyone believed the lame

explanations your tried to sell, do you? We all knew it was smoke. Ask your friends in the Klan. They'll tell you there was no question what your actions have been saying for years. I'm surprised the NAACP hasn't asked you to return that award they gave you."

I winced visibly, and Abe noticed.

"I didn't say that to make you feel bad, Congressman. I know you're frustrated with your Party. You've said publicly it's been pulled off center. The truth, however, is that—as least as far as being the Party of Lincoln goes— you've gone completely off the rails, into no man's land and found your way back to the 1950s. You of *all* people know that. So please stop embarrassing yourself by referring to the G.O.P. that way."

Being reminded of the award I received when I was CEO made me feel ashamed. Again, it pointed to something I'd somehow stopped appreciating when I moved out of business and into politics. We'd worked very hard not just to have a diverse workforce but to make our culture welcoming to everyone. It was obvious it was the smart thing to do for every possible reason— legal, ethical, and financial. Anytime I got pushback about new hires who supposedly didn't 'fit in' because they were racially or sexually 'different,' I'd simply ask, "So you're telling me I should fire them, let them work for our competitor, and watch *their* share price go up while ours

42

tanks?" That always did it.

"Point taken," I said.

He simply nodded. He knew I'd conceded.

"But this sort of thing is so much more complicated to manage in politics," I explained. "It's important that you believe me when I say the people I work with in the Republican party are not closet racists. It's true that the far right has gotten more than a toehold in the party. That faction has gotten aggressive and combative in a way I don't approve of. And maybe the party wasn't as sensitive as we could have been about the optics of taking such a hard line with our first African-American President. But if genuine racists chose to misread our intentions, that was out of our control. I'm not going to deny some of the unfortunate consequences of such a misunder-standing. If it turns out—"

He burst out laughing. *"Optics? Misunderstandings?* Damn, you've developed a truly amazing capacity for rationalizing poor behavior." He shook his head in astonishment and took a few steps while he mumbled to himself.

He held up one finger. "You yelled 'fire' by demonizing the President and making people feel he was a threat."

Then a second finger. "You *failed* to yell 'fire' when you tolerated the racist messages. You let all sorts of lies go unchallenged which encouraged people who were easily manipulated to believe that the President was their enemy."

A third. "You were hypocrites in treating President Obama in a way you'd never consider treating any white President. You changed the rules just to get something you wanted.

"And if those aren't bad enough, I don't even know how to describe your colossal moral failure when it came to PizzaGate."

My heart sank. This was probably the *last* thing I wanted to talk about when it came to *respect*. He read this in a flash. I could tell he was going to grind me into dust.

"I'm sure you and I would agree there's a special place in Hell for pedophiles. Yes?"

I simply nodded.

"They're vile individuals who deserve no mercy. Correct?"

I nodded again.

"So, what's the right thing to do when we suspect children are being targeted by someone? And silence won't do on this, Congressman. What should we do?"

"Notify the authorities."

"You mean the police."

"Yes."

"Why?"

"Because it's a serious crime."

"Right. A serious crime. And how sure do we have to be before we go to the authorities?"

"We definitely need reason to suspect something wrong is happening. Then we trust that the police will do their job and look into it."

"But since this is so serious a matter, why don't we just broadcast as widely as possible that the person we suspect is a pedophile?"

"I would prefer not to discuss this."

He snorted. "Do you think I'm a reporter that you can just stonewall and shoo away? This is serious business, Congressman, and not optional." His voice had that steely quality again. "Why not just go public with our suspicions?"

I walked a few steps and decided to take my medicine.

"That's obvious. If we're wrong, we could ruin someone's life. That's a terrible thing to accuse someone of if it's false."

"I'm sorry. I'm not sure I heard you correctly. Would you repeat that for me?"

He'd heard me perfectly well and was just twisting the knife. But my shame kept me from pushing back.

"It's a terrible accusation. It could ruin someone's life."

"And I'm sure you and I would agree that anyone who made such an unfounded accusation would be a vicious, sick bastard. Yes?"

"Yes."

"So, if we take *respect* seriously, what should we do when we suspect someone's being falsely accused of such a terrible crime?"

"We should speak out and defend them," I murmured.

"Louder, Congressman."

"OK! I did nothing! I knew I should have. Everyone in the Party knew we should have. We were cowards who didn't want to piss off the far-right."

"Yes," he responded calmly. "Cowards. A bunch of vicious, sick bastards shout from the rooftops that Hillary Clinton and John Podesta are running a child sex ring out of a pizza place in D.C. In response, you, Comrade Pinocchio, and your Congressional compadres say nothing because the people targeted are in the other party. *Nothing!*

"Of course, all of you finally have to react when some guy shows up to rescue the children allegedly being victimized. He grabbed that *assault rifle* you let him buy, drove to D.C., fired off a few rounds, and will spend four years in prison for ... what? Being too stupid to realize that fascists don't give a crap about the people who believe the filth they spread?

"Your party's thrown in its lot with vicious, self-serving propagandists, Congressman. Face it. If you honestly believed in treating everyone with respect, your job was to do whatever you could to stop the spread of such a despicable accusation. Instead, you did what you seem to have a real knack for—nothing."

He stopped and quietly let me marinate in my shame.

"Let me put this as simply as I can. Even if it's true that you and other members of your party aren't racists, fascists, or pathological liars, you don't mind getting their votes. Worse still, you don't give people who traffic in fear, bias, and hatred any reason to vote *against* you. After all, if you're a true champion of the values on which this country is based, you should be *offending* these people every day—certainly often enough that they don't vote for you.

"If you think this is just *optics* and *misunderstandings*, you really have forgotten what was obvious to you as a CEO. And if that's the person you've become, I can promise you'll go down in flames in the election. We'll make sure of it. History is on our side. We have the wind at our backs—and a huge war chest. Your party got so enamored with gerrymandering you've ignored that the people you've been kicking around make up *the majority*. But we're taking America back, and my group is giving you a chance to be a patriot. We want to help you remember your true self. I believe he's still inside there somewhere. So, do you and I stop talking, or do we continue?"

I felt unfairly lumped together with people I genuinely believed were little better than pond scum. And I didn't appreciate being threatened by my companion when he surely understood the compromises I had to make to stay in office. But every time he referred to my time as CEO, I felt a twinge of guilt. He was right. I'd supported 'party positions' I would have thought were wrong and self-destructive when I was in business. I'd tolerated and remained silent about behavior I thought was disgraceful because it was politically expedient. This conversation was making me more unsettled than I'd expected.

"You're thinking, not punching back. I like that. I'm sure that you and many other 'mainstream Republicans' are heartsick over what's done in the name of the G.O.P. And I'm serious when I say we want to help you. But you've got to start being honest with yourself about how you've made things worse by your inaction. For now, the question is just whether we continue talking."

I swallowed hard. "I understand what you're charging both me and my party with, and I'm not going to argue with you. You've pointed out some things I was already disappointed in myself about. I'd like to mull over some of the things you said. I suggest that we agree to discuss this in the future. For now, I propose we move on to one of the other values your group supports."

He nodded approvingly. "A man willing to ruminate about things. Gold star, Congressman. So, on to our next topic."

We took a few more steps.

"So far, you've failed to measure up in terms of three of the ideas we started with. Feel like seeing how you punt another as well—where you deny that $1 + 1 + 1 + 1 = 4$? In fact, you say it equals zero."

CHAPTER THREE

I laughed. After his somber comments about *respect*, it felt like we'd gone from tragedy to comedy. Maybe this would at least be entertaining. "You're telling me I can't do arithmetic. That I've added 1 +1 +1 +1 and come up with 0?" I was curious about what he had up his sleeve. "Do you honestly think I could have gotten to where I am if I couldn't handle something as simple as 1 +1+ 1 + 1?"

He cocked an eyebrow. "On the contrary, maybe your *failure* to do so is the secret of your success."

It wasn't a compliment.

He pointed to a bench, motioning we should sit. "As I said, I want to give you the benefit of the doubt. Show me again what 1 + 1 + 1 + 1 equals. Use your business cards, like before"

I knew this was the start of another maneuver to put the screws to me, but unless I was going to walk away, I needed to cooperate. I dutifully took out four cards and placed them in front of him, one at a time. "One ... plus one … plus one … plus one … equals … one, two, three, *four.*"

"Are you positive?" He smirked. He was enjoying himself too much. This was obviously a trap. "Absolutely sure? Positively certain? You have no doubt at all? We can take this to the bank?"

I hesitated. I was being set up, but I couldn't figure out what he was trying to pull.

"Yes. Absolutely, positively, certainly, undoubtedly bankable."

"Excellent. *Why?*"

"What do you mean, 'Why'?"

"Why are you so certain?"

"It's obvious."

"Of course, it's obvious *to me*. But I'm not the one with the problem. That's why I need you to explain why you're sure it's 4."

Definitely being set up.

"You enjoy these little stunts, don't you? And then, when you get people where you want them, turning the knife?"

He grinned and said nothing. He just waited for me to continue. It was like we were playing chess, and it was my move.

"Fine. It's 4 because *we can see it*. The fact that one card plus one card plus one card plus one card equals *four* cards is right before our eyes."

When the corner of his mouth inched up, I knew I'd stepped into his snare.

"Did you just say it's a *fact?*"

"Yes. See?" I pointed at the cards again. "One, two, three, *four*. It's a fact."

"Hmmm. You did it *again*." He stroked his chin, shook his head and put on his phoniest 'I'm really puzzled' face as he studied the cards.

"OK, what's the deal? What did I do *again?*" He wasn't going to make this easy for me.

"You called it *a fact*."

"So?"

"You don't believe in facts."

"Are you crazy? Of course, I believe in facts."

"No, you don't."

"Yes, I do."

"No, you don't."

"Y—" I paused. The expression on his face said he was willing to go back and forth like this forever. "Fine, I'll bite. What makes you say I don't believe in facts?"

He smiled as he put the tablet he'd been carrying onto the bench. He touched the screen, and images of the backs of five playing cards appeared. Four were connected by 'plus signs.' Then an 'equals' sign led to the fifth. He pointed to the first four.

"One plus one plus one plus one ..." Then he pointed to the fifth, "equals *four*. ... Well, actually *1.7*, but we'll get to that. When *you* add up these cards, however, you come up with *zero*."

I shook my head at how nonsensical this was. "No. I know there are *four* cards there. ... 1.7?"

"Perhaps it would help if I said, "This *fact* plus this *fact* plus this *fact* plus this *fact*." He pointed to each card. "Equals *this* fact." He pointed to the fifth. "It's simple. If you touch the images, the cards turn over."

There was a different graph on each of them. I understood what he was up to. Clever.

"I just see a bunch of squiggly lines."

"You aren't going to finesse your way out so easily, Congressman. You see *facts.*"

He pointed to the cards one at a time.

"The increase in atmospheric carbon dioxide over the last half-century ...

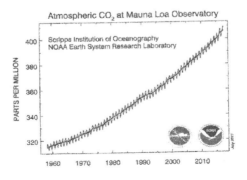

plus the relationship between CO2 and global temperature ...

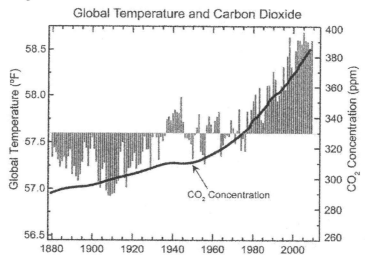

combined with ice core data about the relationship between global temperature ...

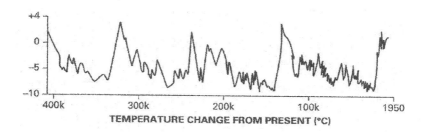

and CO2 concentrations over the last 400,000 years ...

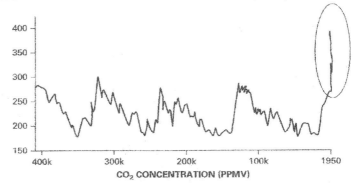

show that the 1.7 degree increase in global temperature since industrialization

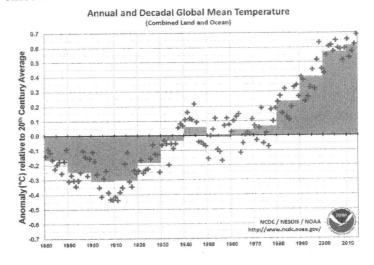

is real, serious, and the result of human activity.

Those are *facts*, Congressman. However, you deny

them. When you look at these facts, you say, '1 +1 +1 + 1 equals *zero*—ZERO global climate change.' You belong to the party of climate change deniers. Remember?"

"Hold it. I never *denied* climate change. Whenever I'm asked, I say I'm not a scientist and that my understanding of things is there's no consensus among scientists. I've read that even some Nobel prize winning physicist is a skeptic. So, I think the prudent thing for a politician like me is to wait and see."

He gave me the most bemused look.

"Do me a favor. Repeat that."

I thought I'd been clear enough, but I was willing to say it again. He wore the same expression the whole time I spoke. He apparently found my answer entertaining.

"Remarkable. Exactly the same way both times. Same inflections. Same rhythm. And with such sincerity. I'm sure your constituents believe you. Hell, *you* probably believe you."

He scratched his beard, looked off into the distance and grimaced. Then he turned my way again. "Horse piss."

"Excuse me?" He had a talent for making no sense.

"I'm sorry. Was I being crude? Should I have said 'horse *urine*?"

"You should explain to me why you've decided to insult me again. I thought you were big on *respect*."

He snorted. "From where I sit, *you're* the one who's

reverted to being insulting with that ridiculous 'I'm not a scientist' crap. I thought that meant we were playing, 'Who can sound most like a Faux-Republican?' Aren't the *new rules* that whenever we're wrong, we say something stupid, irrelevant, or trash each other? We yell, 'Fake news!' 'Alternative facts!' ... 'Tone from the top,' eh?"

He was like a dog with a bone.

"Come on, Congressman. Be honest. Your 'I'm not a scientist' remark is nothing more than a dance so you don't offend anyone. It's not a serious reply to the evidence.

"You want to go back to talking about *respect?* Fine. What kind of respect does that show to the thousands of climate scientists around the world who have documented a threat to the future of *your children and grandchildren?* What kind of respect does it show to say, 'Sorry, kid. There are all kinds of serious problems on the way because of global warming—food, water, disease, population disruption. It's going to affect your generation more than mine. But my party decided to make political hay by denying science. Good luck solving a problem you had no hand in creating.' What do you think your *grandchildren* will say to you if your party gets its way on this or any of your plans to assault the environment? '*Thank you*, grandpa?' Ha! More likely, '*Fuck you*, grandpa!'"

He sighed and shook his head. "Like I said, *horse piss!*"

He picked up his tablet from the bench, and we continued walking along the Mall. I grumbled to myself.

"Fine. I admit it was a politically motivated answer. Let me remind you. Tough primary. Pushed by the radical right. You would have preferred that my opponent won?"

He rolled his eyes dramatically. "Heaven forbid!"

"I'm taking that as a resounding 'no.'"

"Yes, Congressman. That's a 'no.' I'd much rather discuss this with you. I wouldn't have wasted my time with the idiot you beat. He can't hold a candle to you. You have huge potential. I was genuinely happy that you won that race."

"Thank you for that much, at least." I appreciated hearing it.

"Still ..."

I looked at him askance. "There's no stopping you, is there? You just couldn't graciously concede that I did my best in a bad situation."

"You're right." Then after a few more paces ...

"Still ..."

I couldn't help but laugh.

"Fine. Out with it."

"It's true that you *aren't* a scientist, but you've cast lots of votes on issues that involved science. It never bothered you before. Your position on global warming is the combination of barefaced intellectual dishonesty and sucking up to voters the Faux-G.O.P. had already duped.

"And while some physicist may be a skeptic, that's irrelevant. You didn't mention that *ninety-seven percent of climate scientists* agree. They're the experts. And there's virtual unanimity among them. Don't you respect specialists?"

"But the Nobel Prize winner. You can't ignore so prominent a scientist."

"I can, and so should you. He's a physicist, not a climate scientist. Tell me this, when you were a CEO, what kind of background did your director of operations have?"

"She was a mechanical engineer."

"But what if an electrical engineer visited your plant one day and said the mechanical engineer was all wrong?"

"It wouldn't make any difference. Mechanical engineering isn't his specialty."

"But he's an *engineer*, nonetheless."

I shrugged my shoulders. He was right.

"The *facts* are there, Congressman, no matter how much your party wants to deny them. What do you tell the people who live in Miami Beach about the 'sunny day flooding' they now experience? That because it *can't* be caused by rising sea levels from global warming, it must be excessive humidity?

"The scientific evidence for global climate change has

been so obvious to experts that the matter was settled when the first reports of the Intergovernmental Panel on Climate Change came out *in the 1990s!* The evidence has been in *for almost thirty years.* It's been recognized by virtually every other country on the planet. But *your party* says '*No! No!* It's a myth made up by that Muslim terrorist Barack Obama!' Do you feel *proud* of the Faux-G.O.P.'s disdain for *facts* and *science*?

"And to make matters worse, your party didn't just fail to warn people of a serious threat. You and your friends in the petroleum industry told them *there was nothing to worry about.* But that was a lie, wasn't it? There *will* be harm from climate change, Congressman. Hell, there already has been! And the longer your party denies the facts, the more responsible you are for it."

By now we were in front of the Air and Space Museum. "The achievements honored inside that building—everything from the Wright Brothers to landing on the moon—were the result of the scientific discovery of *facts.* I imagine that if your crowd held sway during the 1960s, the Soviets would have planted the first flag on the moon. And while your guy would have loved that, it wouldn't have made the rest of us very happy.

He stopped and turned to me. "You're intelligent. On such a serious threat as global warming, why didn't you take the time to look into the scientific evidence from the

IPCC yourself before saying something? Or did you shut off your brain when you stopped being CEO and decide propaganda was good enough?"

He held his arms high and wide as though he was making important pronouncements. "This just in! Climate change is a hoax! Billions of illegal votes in the last election! Barack Obama is the anti-Christ! Boosting corporate profits will provide jobs in the U.S.! The more unregulated the economy is, the better! Lower taxes are always good! Wealth at the top trickles down. A rising tide floats all boats! Corporate profits mean more jobs!' Or maybe you get your facts from Comrade Pinocchio?" He poked me hard on the shoulder and started walking again.

I didn't appreciate being called on the carpet and pushed around. But I couldn't deny that our conversation was reminding me how uneasy I was with how I handled a number of issues. I also had the sense that every now and then he deliberately tried to provoke me. I wasn't going to let him succeed. He'd made his point about climate change. Yes, I knew there were scientific facts supporting the idea. But I honestly didn't know the climate science community had come to a consensus. I just found a way to finesse the issue in a tough election because that's what a key voting block wanted to hear. I bet that if Abe ever had to run for office, he'd be singing a different tune about how candid you can be in a tough race. As far as I was concerned, we were done with this topic. I waited to hear what we'd discuss next.

"Silence, Congressman? You're good at that, aren't you?" He glanced down at me. "Maybe you handed over your balls as well as your brain. You said barely a discouraging word about Comrade Pinocchio during your campaign. 'People cheered as the Twin Towers collapsed.' 'Barack Obama's not an American.' 'Climate change is a Chinese hoax.' 'I know more than the generals.' 'It was just locker room talk.' 'Murder rates are up.' 'Life in the inner cities is Hell.' 'Millions of illegal votes were cast.' 'Reporters are the most dishonest people on earth.' 'Immigrants from the Middle East are dangerous.' 'The Russians didn't mess with our election.' *Lies! All lies!* Offered without a shred of evidence! And barely a peep from you—either during the campaign or since. Your silence speaks volumes, Congressman. Horse piss! For *both* of you!"

If my daughter were here, she would have kissed Abe. She's an idealistic, energetic college student. She badgered me incessantly about my staying silent. But she's naïve about how the world works. I wasn't happy saying nothing about behavior I personally found repugnant. It was the only way I could keep my seat. But to be honest, I was finding it harder to live with the longer I talked to Abe.

"OK," I said seriously, "I'll check out the evidence for climate change."

He nodded. "You're a gentleman. Your word is good enough for me. Shall we change topics?"

I was glad he backed off. Now it gave me a chance to move our discussion to something on my turf. He'd slipped up when he said something a couple of minutes ago, and I wanted to turn the tables. "Sure, but before that, you need to explain why you labeled as propaganda *basic economic facts* everyone knows are tr—"

He put his hand on my shoulder. "Oh, I'm sorry to interrupt. One more *small* point about global warming I almost forgot," he said offhandedly. "When you're checking out the evidence, be sure you read that report about the connection between climate change and international terrorism.

"Now, you started saying something about the economy? Please continue."

I stopped in mid-step as he casually strolled along. I'm sure he was smirking. I should have known he was giving up too easily. But this seemed way over the top. Climate change and terrorism? I hurried to catch up with him.

"You need to explain that."

He stopped and looked my way. "No. I don't think so."

"Wait. You drop a bombshell like that and refuse to

explain it?"

"That's right. Why, does it bother you?

"Of course, it does. It's infuriating."

He gave me another one of his phony 'I'm puzzled' looks.

"But isn't that another of the *new Republican rules?* If we don't feel like answering something, we don't. We basically just tell the person asking the question to go screw themselves. I'm just being like one of your G.O.P. colleagues."

He couldn't resist twisting the knife.

"Look, Congressman, I've told you enough to show that you and your cronies are happy putting your heads in the sand. This is one topic you going to take responsibility for learning about if you want the facts. I'll simply tell you that there's a report by a group of retired Admirals and Generals that connects the dots between climate change and terrorism. Hopefully, you have enough confidence in our military to trust *them* more than you trust left-wing, conspiracy mongering, grant hungry scientists."

I was stunned. He was serious about the connection.

He continued. "How do I put this politely? I'm not giving you the details because it's time for you to wake up out of your fog, get off your ass, do some work, and realize you've been conned by your party leaders. ... So, the economy?"

I was baffled that I'd heard none of this from the party's national security hawks. If the *military* was convinced—

"The economy, Congressman," he interrupted. "Or we move to the next item on *my* list."

It took a few moments for me to shift gears. I forced myself to focus. "OK, everybody knows those things about the economy you said were *propaganda* are true. Even *you* know that. Wealth *does* trickle down and benefits people farther down in the economy. Lower corporate taxes *do* translate into jobs. So, what was the point? Were you just seeing if I was listening to you?"

He started to say something but swallowed his words. At first, I thought he'd choked on having to admit he was wrong. When I looked at his face, however, I realized it would have been another "horse piss!" He pointed to a bench, and we sat down.

"Those aren't *facts*, Congressman, because they aren't true. They're *beliefs*—and *false* beliefs at that. They're part of your economic and political religion. If they were facts, *this* would be impossible."

He punched his tablet and brought up some images.

"Here's the U.S. GDP since 1950.

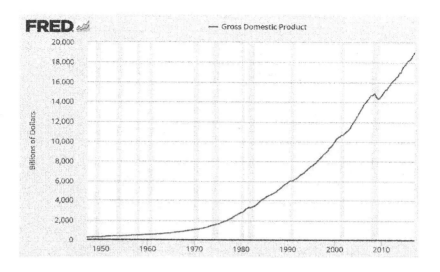

And here's the Dow Jones during the same period.

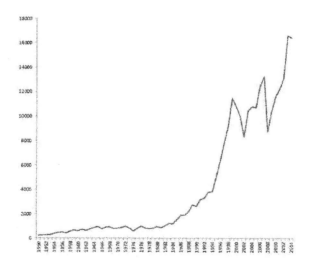

Except for the occasional dip, that never lasts very

long, we see a nice, steady increase. Correct?"

I studied the images. "Right."

He brought up another graph.

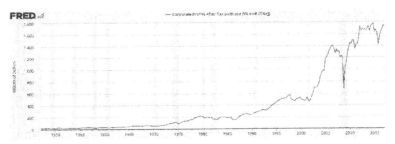

"This shows corporate profits over the same time period. Again, it tracks up. Good news, right?"

"True."

Then he brought up another. "*This* is the problem."

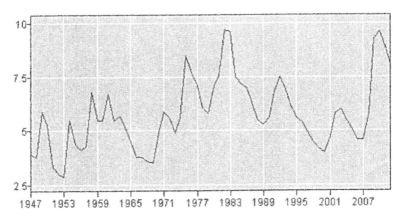

It was a very different sort of line. Up and down, sometimes dramatically so. "This is unemployment for the same period. And remember that the official

68

unemployment figures were low. By some accounts, the real number was almost 20% in parts of the country. If what you say is true—that wealth trickles down and that corporate success translates into jobs—this shouldn't look like this. There shouldn't be periods of major unemployment at the same time companies are doing so well."

"And what about wages? There should be good news on that, right? But there isn't. In fact, throughout the recovery after the meltdown, while the stock market and corporate profits went up, wages were flat. Actually, they've been worse than flat. They've been dropping as a percentage of the economy. See?"

He swiped the screen again.

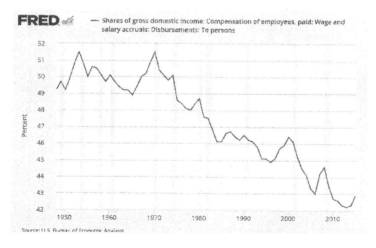

"Meanwhile, the income gains for the top 1% dramatically outstripped everyone else's."

Income Gains at the Top Dwarf Those of Low- and Middle-Income Households

Percent change in real after-tax income since 1979

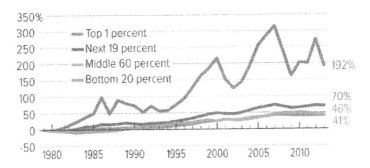

"So, do me a favor. Show me the 'trickling down' to average working people."

I stared at the charts and didn't know what to say. As CEO, I spent a lot of time making my way through the complex numbers connected with running a significant company. But I focused on quarter to quarter. I might glance at the latest reports about S&P or GDP, but I never stepped back and looked at economic trends that spanned decades. The numbers were plain. Virtually all the wealth—massive amounts—floated to the top. Ordinary working people—like my former employees—were getting even less of the pie than they were 30 years ago.

Then he brought up one of the earlier graphs and circled the last big dip.

"Recognize this?"

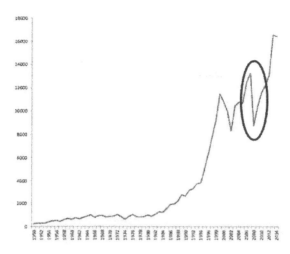

Sadly, I did. "The 2008 crash."

"Made possible by more of your sacred truths. 'Government regulation of Wall Street is bad!' 'The free market will regulate things.' If the market could be trusted so much, Congressman, how did *10 trillion* dollars of wealth evaporate? For a party that has traditionally been 'pro-business,' how did your policies let us get to the edge of global financial disaster? At least Alan Greenspan admitted he was wrong. But as far as I can tell, you and your cronies have just dug in and continue to sing the same old song. What's the deal? You didn't do enough damage the last time you gave the banks free rein?"

I was uncomfortable feeling so defensive on a topic I felt I owned.

"OK," I admitted, "the market doesn't operate *perfectly*. But you're oversimplifying a complicated problem that was driven by lots of factors. No verification mortgages. The ratings agencies. *Way* too much speculation in real estate that led to an overheated market. The—"

"You're right," he conceded. "There's plenty of blame to go around. *But* ... your version of how the economy works assumes at the very least that a free market economy won't blow itself up. In real life, however, people operated in a way that led to their own financial devastation." He pointed to the tablet again. "These *facts* don't support your version of how the economy works."

He kept on talking, but I stopped listening. I'd taken the tablet from him and was scrolling through the graphs. He had to be leaving something out. If you'd given me all the 'good news' graphs and asked what to describe what was happening in the rest of the economy, I would have said a healthy job market and rising incomes. What he showed me should have been impossible. But his facts looked accurate.

"And one final point ..."

Even though I wasn't listening to him carefully, this broke through. When I looked up at him, he was chuckling. "I figured that would get your attention. Look, I know I'm throwing a lot at you that goes against what, for most of your life, you've been sure was true about how the economy operated. But this is incredibly important if we want to remain a democracy. For example, my group believes that the failure of the economy to distribute wealth more fairly has produced a fundamental threat to freedom."

"A threat to freedom? You can't be serious? It's exactly the opposite. All that new wealth is testimony to free-market entrepreneurship and the creation of new industries."

"You're looking at trees, not the forest, Congressman. Yes. New companies and new industries have sprung into existence. There are some great success stories—your company's among them. But you're ignoring the oligarchs."

The way Abe shot off in a totally new direction with no explanation was really annoying. "Oligarchs? What do the Russians have to do with this?"

He looked at me and sighed disappointedly.

"The *American* oligarchs," he said patiently. "The richest 10% now control 75% of the nation's wealth, and their share continues to grow. The top 1% alone controls 30 to 40%. In a capitalistic economy, wealth means *power*. So, your party's tax policies have systematically transferred not just wealth, but *power* to a tiny minority of the citizenry."

He looked at me sharply. "You know, you people are always ready to decry concentrations of power when it comes to the *government*. But you happily ignore concentrations of *economic* power. Why is that,

Congressman? Does your crowd not see it, which makes you *stupid?* Or you do you see it and not care, which makes you *hypocrites?* Or do you see it and like it, which makes you *proto-fascists*, looking for any way to be able to push people around?"

I ground my teeth at the insult. I wasn't going to take the bait this time. I got up and walked away. He caught up with me, stood right in front of me, and looked down with a scowl on his face. "I didn't hear an answer, Congressman. Is your party's mascot Bozo, Janus, or Hitler?"

Seeing red, I spun around and walked away again. I was tired of Abe's self-indulgent rants. I groaned when I heard him catch up with me.

"Well done, grasshopper."

Damn. Another test.

I stopped and looked at him. "Has anyone ever told you how annoying you can be?"

"I don't suppose you'd believe me if I said, 'no,' would you?"

I just laughed.

"Seriously. Excellent self-control."

"That was just a stunt to provoke me, right? There no American oligarchs?"

"No stunt. I'm serious. Concentrations of money mean concentrations of power. *Massive* concentrations of power threaten freedom and democracy. But let's make that part of your homework—more facts to research."

I brooded over what he'd just said as we walked along. Abe and I saw the world so differently, I was beginning to think there was too big a gap between us to bridge. I also didn't like his constantly insulting tone. He seemed to sense what my silence meant.

"Congressman, I appreciate that what you're hearing is tough to take in. But I believe that, in the end, you and I are more alike than different. If I didn't think that, we wouldn't be having this conversation. The only people I argue hard against are those I respect. And while you may doubt it, I both like and respect you. I just want you to wake up out of the fog you've been in. My group thinks you've forgotten important things you used to know. We're hoping you'll remember enough of them to realize you've been pulled away from what you believe in your heart and that you'll want to join us.

"We think you can be a positive force in this country. As I said, we aren't partisan. But we're massively unhappy with the way values we consider vital to the health of the country have been undermined by your party. As you gathered from where you and I started, we think that *respect* is key. But so is *intelligence*. And whatever the Faux-G.O.P. is the 'party of ...,' Congressman, it isn't the party of intelligence. Call us crazy, but we think a species that calls itself the 'thinking hominid' should actually *think!* It should *value* intelligence not undermine it.

"You're a smart guy. You graduated *summa* from Michigan and went on for a MBA. You're universally admired for turning your company around by using your *brain* and focusing on data. But who are your colleagues now? Serial liars. People who deny evolution and climate science. The carnival barkers who try to sell us the idea of 'alternative facts.' The faithful of the Church of the Free Market who refuse to recognize the risks of Wall Street greed and insanity. My God! One of your guys claimed that evolution and the Big Bang are 'lies straight from the pit of Hell.' And another said, 'If it's a legitimate rape, the female body has ways to try to shut the whole thing down'! My group honestly feels that your gang is carrying out an assault on reason itself."

I winced at the list he ticked off. Even I recognized it as a litany of my party's sins.

"Your party leaders have no compunction doing things they would have screamed to high heaven about if the other side did. Consistency is the 'hobgoblin of little minds'? You scream like banshees about 'the deficit!' until you get into power. Then $1 trillion is pocket change! You people are shameless. You treat *logic* as a disease to be crushed out.

"God! When I hear the lies, the 'special rules,' the

rationalizations—all delivered with a straight face—it feels like my sanity's being attacked. It looks to us like you've decided the best way your party can stay in power is to make ignorance and gullibility a virtue. 'G.O.P.'? No. 'D.A.F.'

He stopped and looked at me with all the sincerity and concern of a close friend. "Look, Stephen, I don't mean to insult you personally. I know I sound angry. And I am—but not at you. I'm mad at the proto-fascists who have taken over your party and have been pulling your strings. With you, I'm *frustrated*, not angry." He sighed. He looked at me intently. "I ... You ... We ... The problem ...," he sputtered, unable to get even *part* of a sentence out. He laughed at himself. "I'm so frustrated, I can't find the words that capture what I want to say to you."

I chuckled. "You? Lost for words? That's got to be a first. OK, just spit it out."

"Let me apologize in advance for being so crude. But ... what the *fuck* are you doing associating with that crowd? You're better than that. You know it. I know it. The country deserves you, but they don't. Let me help you." I was startled at how blunt, genuine, passionate, and personal his plea was. I was also flattered.

"Feel better?"

He laughed.

We walked again, and he let his comments sink in. He was right. I didn't feel like the people in my party were really my 'tribe' anymore. I kept going back to Abe's remark that there were things I knew as a CEO that I'd forgotten after a few years in politics. How you treat people—no matter how much you disagree with them. And that the point of having a brain is to use it to solve problems—not to manipulate, brow beat, lie or deceive to advance some narrow interest. At my company, we had a big sign in each conference room that said, 'We're here to solve problems and make the world a better place.' That wasn't the attitude that predominated in party meetings. It was about party loyalty, an extremist ideology, identifying and attacking enemies, winning and losing. It hit me that being at my company felt like 'home.' That was *not* the case in my Congressional caucus.

"Your party's trying to get people to shut off the higher parts of their brain and be governed by emotions, not reason. And not just any emotion—*fear*. Fear there's some dark threat out there that only you can protect them from. Fear of people who look different. Fear that if we wait to determine whether it's true that someone or something is a threat, disaster will happen. Better to strike first than to regret we waited. *Fear*. But I don't need to lecture you about that, Congressman, do I? Your party's been fear-mongering so well for years that you paved the way for Comrade Pinocchio.

"The Faux-G.O.P. has painted anyone who disagrees with its policies as an enemy motivated by hatred for America. They say their opponents want to take away everyone's guns, deny religious liberty, destroy a traditional way of life. Even scientists get targeted. They aren't doing their jobs as researchers. They're conning the public so they can get research grants. Ordinary civil servants who put 'climate change' into their reports get fired as though they're engaged in sedition.

"*Reason*, not emotion, is the chief trait that got us where we are as a species. Reason lets us determine what's true and false. We solve problems with it. Our brains let us discover that the planet really is warming up and that we need to do something about it."

He poked me in the arm. I knew he couldn't resist going back to that.

"Intelligence stops us from doing things that are either stupid—like jumping off a cliff believing that if we flap our arms we'll fly—or terrible—attacking someone with a different skin color or religion from ours because it makes us feel safer."

His passion about this topic was so strong, this was obviously a hot button. The best thing for me to do was to wait until he'd let off all the steam.

"Ultimately, reason and intelligence are as important

for protecting our freedom as the military. Our armed forces protect us from external threats. But we need reason, intelligence, and education to protect us from internal dangers.

"People who want to take away your liberty prefer you to be stupid. That way, they can fool you with their lies and propaganda. They manipulate you into doing something that you regret only when it's too late.

"The way we see it, Congressman, the country's in danger of becoming so self-destructively stupid, we're starting to hand it over to the enemies of what 'America' truly stands for. Your party has been paving the way to that for at least the last 20 years. And you've got to stop being part of that."

I wanted to feel insulted. That was a terrible thing to say about any political party. And he said it about *mine*. But his voice was filled with such overwhelming, heartfelt sadness, all I could feel was sympathy for his pain.

I scrambled to respond with an intelligent defense. But I couldn't find one. Abe was right in saying the G.OP. had been pulled to a place where ideology was more important than facts. In business, I was a hard-nosed 'facts-numbers-data guy.' My attitude was we either knew something or we didn't. If we had to make a decision about something, everybody knew that if they wanted to persuade me to go a certain way, they had to lead with the facts. That was something else I'd apparently forgotten after doing time in Congress.

"Want to tally up how your party did in this round?" He began counting off on his fingers.

"One. Denying climate science. Passing off your economic ideology as the key to prosperity, when it's anything *but*. Screaming 'government regulation is bad and the markets can regulate themselves!' ... So, you regularly fail to warn people of genuine threats. That looks to me like *not* yelling 'Fire' when there's a conflagration coming our way.

"Two. It isn't just that you refuse to see how facts 'add up.' The Faux-G.O.P. is so allergic to the truth and so contemptuous of reason that, in your world, '1 + 1 + 1 + 1' equals 'a blue hat that can talk.' That's what little sense your crowd makes. Yet you all say it so seriously, you con those who are easy to fool. You aren't a bunch of idiots, so you must know what you're doing. Like I said before— barefaced intellectual dishonesty."

He turned as we got to a crosswalk and hit the button for the pedestrian crossing. He took a deep breath, looked at me and smiled. "End of tirade ... at least for now." When the light changed, he strode across the street. "There's a coffee place just a few blocks away. Let's take a break."

"Finally," I laughed, "something I can agree with!"

Once we crossed the street, curiosity got the best of me. *"Horse piss?"* I asked. "That's the best an elegant, sophisticated, public-spirited gentleman can do." After the way he'd lectured me, he deserved a poke.

He laughed. "OK. Maybe not the most polite response. But the way politicians of all stripes play fast and loose with language, truth, and reason makes me crazy. The dodges, half-truths, outright lies. If it were up to me, every time some officeholder or candidate did that, he or she should be made to drink horse piss as a reminder of how offensive what just came out of their mouth was. So, that's why my reply to your 'I'm not a scientist' explanation about climate change was 'horse piss.'"

He smirked and hopped up on the nearest bench. Then he shielded his eyes from the sun, squinted, and scanned the horizon in every direction. "Why is it that you can never find a horse when you really need one?" he added with a wink.

"Smart ass."

He just grinned. "Something else we agree on."

CHAPTER FOUR

We entered the coffee shop and got our drinks. While there were plenty of empty tables around us, Abe motioned that I should follow him up the stairs to the next level. "It's quieter." He was right. It was completely empty and definitely more conducive to conversation. We sank into a couple of overstuffed chairs and put our drinks on the marble topped table.

"So, *life*."

"I'm sorry. *Life?*"

"The next value on my list. We started with *respect*, then different facets of *reason*—truth, logic, intelligence, intellectual honesty. Where do you stand on *life?*"

After being pushed around in our conversation so far, I was relieved to hear where he wanted to go next. I was positive we were on the same page on this one.

"I'm sure you know that throughout my entire stint in Congress I've been an unflinching defender of the right to life. Abortion is a terrible tragedy, and we have to do everything we can to protect the sanctity of life. It's regrettable when women find themselves with unwanted pregnancies, and, on virtually every other matter, I'd say that the individual's right to choose their actions is sacred and shouldn't be compromised by government interference. But this is a special case. Abortion ends an innocent human life. And we simply can't allow that in this country. I'm sure you agree."

His frown told me that, again, I'd misjudged something.

"Why is it one step forward then two steps back with you, Congressman?"

"I don't understand. You said 'life.' What's more important than protecting innocent lives?"

"Nothing. I agree with you."

Now I was really puzzled. "Then I have no idea what your problem is with what I just said."

He sighed. "We agree about the sanctity of life and protecting the innocent. But I was talking about *guns*, not theocracy. Every year, more than 30,000 people die in the U.S. from guns, and we've had one mass murder af—"

"Wait. *Theocracy?* Are you crazy? I didn't say anything like that. And if we agree about the sanctity of life, we have to see abortion the same way—absolutely wrong. We need to outlaw it."

With his elbows on the chair arms, he folded his hands, steepled his index fingers and put them against his lips. He took a couple of slow breaths. Then he sighed. He put his folded hands in his lap. "Fine, you want to talk about abortion. But as far as I'm concerned, that means we're back to talking about *respect*."

"You said *life*. That's the central issue here."

"Maybe to you. But other people see it differently. I did my homework on you, of course. You're a devout Roman Catholic."

"Yes."

"And that's where your opposition to abortion comes from, correct?"

"That's true for me. But there are plenty of pro-lifers who aren't Catholic. Some are even atheists."

"True—although that's the *smallest* segment of the group against it. Moreover, what's behind the opposition to Roe v. Wade isn't just *religious* beliefs, but *conservative* religious beliefs. Or, let me be blunt about this. What's driving this is the desire of conservative religious believers to use the government to impose their theology on the rest of us. Like I said before—theocracy."

"No. You aren't going to pigeon-hole this as the equivalent of something like an extremist attempt to replace the Constitution with sharia or halacha law. It's more like the struggle against slavery. Sometimes laws allow things that are wrong. Religions have a role in taking the lead in those situations and opening people's eyes so those laws can be changed. Moreover, there's a consensus among major religions on this."

He frowned. "Didn't we just finish talking about the importance of *facts*? And now you say the abortion issue is like *slavery*? *All* religions agree on this? There's not even a consensus in your own religion's theology. Didn't you even do your homework on *this*?"

I didn't appreciate being insulted about something I believed so deeply. "Listen. If you ju—"

He held up his hand again. "Let's take this one step at a time," he said patiently. "First, it's *not* like slavery. Good, unbiased science always showed there was no basis for the claim that blacks and women were inferior. Similarly, good, unbiased science does *not* prove that terminating a pregnancy ends the life of a 'person.' I appreciate that your religion may tell you that it is, but that's my point. The basis of that assertion is a specific religious perspective—and not one shared by all religions. Different religions—like different individuals—can look at the same facts and draw different conclusions. I can point you to some Baptist, Lutheran, Jewish, Presbyterian and Methodist discussions that ultimately leave the decision in the hands of the woman and don't argue for making abortion illegal. And then there are the Episcopalians—who show that the Roman Catholic position is a matter of judgment, not something carved in stone in the theology. Which means that, in theory, it can change."

I had no idea what that meant, but I couldn't deny my curiosity. "OK. I'll bite. What do you mean?"

"This is going to take a few minutes to explain, and it's a beautiful day. Let's go back out on the Mall."

In a flash, we were in the sunshine, heading towards the Washington Monument again.

"So, when England's King Henry the Eighth broke with Rome in the sixteenth century, that gave us the Church of England and then its American offshoot—the Episcopalians, right?"

"I take it you live in left field?" I laughed.

"Trust me. This is relevant. Henry. Rome. The Church of England. The Episcopalians?"

"If you say so."

"But that was a totally separate matter from why the Lutherans and Baptists and Presbyterians and all the other Protestant denominations sprung up. Their complaints were *theological*. Henry's break with the Catholic church was *political*. He wanted a divorce. The Pope wouldn't give it to him. So, he said, 'In that case, I'm in charge of the church here in England. Zap! Now I'm divorced.' Virtually everything else—the ceremonies, the sacraments, the priesthood, bishops, the *theology*—stayed the same, especially when you talk about High Church

Anglicans.

The Catholics and Episcopalians start from the same spot, then. But they end up in different places on abortion—as they do on homosexuality and women in the priesthood. The Episcopalians certainly don't say 'anything goes,' but they're not as strict as the Catholics. And this means, as I said, you don't even have a consensus *in your own theology*. Now I'm sure you're going to say something about how the Catholic Church sees itself as the 'one, true faith' and that all the other religions have it wrong. But, of course, the other religions say the same thing. And that's why we have the Establishment Clause of the Constitution."

"What? Slow down. How did you get from theology to the Constitution?"

"I understand you have a portrait of Thomas More in your office. I gather he's something of a hero to you."

"Right. But that has even less to do with what we're talking about?"

"Just tell me why it's there. You'll see."

"I keep it there to remind me of the importance of conscience. *Saint* Thomas More was executed by Henry because he stayed true to his conscience and his faith. But that was at least 250 years before the Constitution. There's no connection."

He sighed. "Let me tell you a few things about your

Saint Thomas More. He was truly a man of the sixteenth century. That means that he shared the idea of the time that heresy was equivalent to sedition and needed to be stamped out. He wrote furiously against Martin Luther. And when he was Lord Chancellor, six heretics were burned at the stake.

"What bothers me most about More, however, is this story. There was a French humanist named Louis de Berquin who was a vocal—and intemperate—critic of the Catholic Church. He occasionally got into trouble with the conservatives, but the King and his sister intervened—until the day Berquin's enemies had him arrested and then burned at the stake as fast as they could. Your *Saint* Thomas More thought that was so great, he called it a miracle brought about by the Blessed Virgin. I cringe every time I think about what he said.

"My point, Congressman, is that the *certainty* religious conviction brings to people can be dangerous. It's a short step from believing God is on your side to taking action against people you're sure are wrong—because you're *positive* that's what God wants. There have been more than 300 acts of anti-abortion violence—arson, bombings, at least 11 deaths. Do you really think that calling abortion 'ending an innocent human life' doesn't spur some people to take action against providers because they think it's God's will? In a country where any wing-nut can get a gun, you can't honestly be surprised by the violence."

We started walking again. He waited to let what he'd told me sink in. I never knew about that side of Thomas More. And I believe so strongly in being true to your conscience—which I admired him for—that I found it deeply troubling he didn't respect that in others.

"And, once again," he continued, interrupting my ruminations, *"that's* why we have the Establishment Clause—which you so casually ignore when you try to force nonbelievers to knuckle under to the rules of your faith. You may not be advocating burning people at the stake or imprisoning them because of their beliefs. But you demonize people who disagree with you with a fanaticism your hero would be proud of. ... Attacking Planned Parenthood? There's a cause to champion!"

His voice was thick with sarcasm.

"Right, let's put an end to all those dangerous, immoral, subversive activities like cancer screenings, STI and pregnancy testing, birth control—because your religion disapproves of a small piece of what they do, while other religions are OK with it. And your party can't even be straightforward about it. No. Those Republican state legislatures pass abortion restrictions in the name of 'women's health'! Horse piss!"

I winced inside. I believe in defending your convictions in an honest, straightforward way. And I wasn't an 'ends justify the means' kind of guy. I was never comfortable with cloaking the real reason for the abortion restrictions. It struck me as cowardly and manipulative.

"OK, Planned Parenthood does some good things, and maybe the restrictions are a smokescreen. But these clinics wouldn't be targets if they simply stopped doing the procedure."

"Because *your* religion says it's wrong. You don't *respect* people enough to think they have a right to different beliefs. There's your theocracy again."

"We aren't imposing anything. It's what the people are asking for through their elected representatives."

He stopped and shook his head in exasperation. "Not only do you fail to realize the danger this poses, but for someone who talks so often about what 'the Founding Fathers' intended, you're astonishingly blind to what they saw so clearly! The brutal and devastating European wars of religion were still going on when people emigrated to the colonies—many for religious liberty. Peace came little more than 100 years before the American Revolution. It was as near to them as World War I is to us. This was recent enough that the Founding Fathers knew how important it was to minimize the social conflict that could be caused by religious strife. That's why religion is supposed to stay out of public policy.

"Look at your *Saint* Thomas More. Look at any religious warrior who is positive they're doing God's work with guns, bombs, and acid. That kind of certainty is dangerous because it lets you inflict cruelty on other people with a clear conscience. And what about the fact that about 60% of people in the country think abortion should be legal? That's a clear *majority*, but you don't care about that. So, when a minority tries to use the government to legislate rules based on religious beliefs, I call that a theocracy."

I turned and faced him. "OK, I admit that other religions look at abortion differently. But this is about religious liberty. People with different beliefs are free to work just as hard as we do to get laws passed that represent their point of view. We're a democracy, after all. The political process protects that."

He started to blurt something out, then caught himself. I was sure it was another "Horse piss!"

"My apologies," he said instead. "Please continue. You were saying this is a matter of religious liberty, Congressman. I agree with you."

I snorted. "No, you don't."

"Yes, I do."

"No, you don't. ... And before we do this forever, now *you* have to explain yourself."

"Fine. I'm talking about religious liberty for *everyone*.

That's why I think this is about *respect*. You and your fellow Catholics should absolutely be free to live according to your belief that abortion is wrong. But you don't have the right to deny religious liberty to *people who disagree with you*. If you get your way, you'd prevent them from living a life in accordance with *their* beliefs. So even though their conscience would be clear ending a pregnancy, you'd force them to go through with it, have the baby, give it up for adoption or raise it. Or maybe you'd drive them to an unsafe back alley abortion. Or, assuming they had the money, you'd make them travel to another country where their beliefs were respected. And if we caught any of them, you'd want them punished, right?"

"Of course not. This isn't a police state. This is America."

"That's right, Congressman. This is America—a country that takes respect seriously. We tolerate differences—*especially* when it comes to religious belief. We cherish individual liberty. You know that famous expression, 'My freedom to move my fist is limited by the location of your chin'? The full expression of *your* religious liberty strikes the chins of lots of other people. That's a dangerous precedent. Are you prepared for the consequences when it's turned against you?"

"Against me?"

"Despite what your crowd maintains, America is not a Christian country or even a Judeo-Christian country. The Constitution doesn't allow for a state religion. So, your position amounts to saying that whichever religion has the most political clout gets to call the tune. Imagine that one or another kind of Great Awakening sweeps the nation. I can think of any number of possibilities where your religion ends up in the crosshairs. There were lots of anti-Catholic fears when Jack Kennedy ran for President. Considering how many Catholics are on the Supreme Court, maybe the authority of the Pope will be seen as a foreign threat again. Or imagine the other end of the religious spectrum. Perhaps a wave of secular humanism aims at closing all religious schools. Do you think your appeal to religious liberty is going to convince anyone? After all, you've changed the rules to make it so that it's just about whoever has enough power to impose their beliefs on everyone else."

He stopped, turned my way and looked at me seriously. "You don't see the danger, do you?" He shook his head. "So, I guess we need to add another category of how your party has failed. This one is *not even seeing a fire when it's heading towards you*." He started to say something then stopped. He stroked his beard and shook his head. "We appear to be at an impasse, Congressman. Let's move on to something else."

I was surprised that he was giving up trying to argue me into the ground. "Sounds reasonable," I said as we started walking again.

"I just want to know why—given your fervent belief in religious liberty—you're so comfortable denying that right to your daughter."

My head snapped his way so quickly I could hear my neck crack. Not only were we *not* changing the subject, he was bringing my daughter into this. I was as angry as I was when he'd mocked my son. I grabbed his arm. "Stop! What's that supposed to mean?"

His eyes narrowed as he looked at my hand squeezing his arm. I let go.

"Calm down, Congressman. I'm not making an accusation or suggesting some dark family secret." He pointed to a bench. "Take a seat."

He waited until we both got settled.

"The first time I mentioned your family, I realized you had a strong protective streak. I admire that. And you've been plain about your commitment to the sanctity of life and desire to protect the innocent. That's all very admirable—but hypocritical."

I realized the reference to Maureen had been another test to see if he could rattle me. Calling me hypocritical was another. This time, I wasn't going to take the bait.

"You're going to have to explain that," I replied

calmly.

He looked impressed that I'd kept my cool.

"Your daughter is away at college. This is her first time living on her own. College is a time for self-discovery—questioning, trying on new roles, deciding what's important in life and who you are. If all you do during that time is live according to your *parents'* values because you think you *should*, they *asked* you to, or, worse yet, they *told* you to, you aren't going to grow into a mature, healthy, independent individual. Part of what young people that age need to do is to decide which moral or spiritual orientation works best for them. That choice should be respected by everyone around them. In America, they have the liberty to worship as they choose—or not to worship at all. Agreed?"

I was at war with myself. It was important to me that my children share my faith. But I'd always encouraged them to think for themselves. I had to accept the possibility they'd see things differently from my wife and me.

"Agreed."

"I have no idea what kind of decisions your daughter is making about her private life. But if she wants advice about sex, birth control or STIs, she's not going to want to talk to her parents or your family physician, who happens to be your wife's tennis partner. And she probably won't go to the university health service. She'd worry that, since it's a Catholic school, she'd get a lecture. In that situation, you want her to get good information and responsible advice, right?"

"Of course."

"If she's lucky, there's an office nearby of that organization you want to shut down—Planned Parenthood."

He waited for me to react. I squirmed, but I wasn't going to give him the satisfaction of provoking me.

He nodded approvingly. "Now let's imagine your worst-case scenario. Your daughter falls in love with a terrific guy on campus. They're crazy about each other. They start having sex, taking all the proper precautions. They end up getting into grad school on opposite sides of the country, however. Neither can imagine life without the other, but both are talented and ambitious. They decide they can handle the distance for a few years, then they'll marry. But just after the first semester of grad school starts, your daughter finds herself pregnant."

He waited again for me to respond. But he knew I didn't know what to say.

"Unlike the crowd you've been hanging around with, Congressman, I believe that, in your heart, you're a sympathetic, compassionate guy. You'd want your daughter to 'do the right thing.' But, given how much is on the line about her future, neither you nor I can know what that is for her. However uncomfortable this may make you, it's possible she'll decide she can't handle a pregnancy at this point in her life—and that the decision to have an abortion is acceptable from her ethical perspective. If so, you'll have to respect that.

"I believe you're a good parent, so you'll want to be supportive. And as much as you disagree with her decision, you'll want her to have good, safe medical care. You may go to your priest later, confess that you feel you've sinned, say your penance and feel remorse about the situation. But I don't think you can look me in the eye and tell me, in that situation, that you'd want your daughter to be living in a country where abortion was illegal. I don't think you can look me in the eye and tell me you'd want her to feel that you were ashamed of her. And I don't think that whenever she looked into a mirror for the rest of her life, you'd want her to see a murderer."

I turned, looked at him said nothing. We both knew he was right.

"Let's walk again. I want to show you something."

I appreciated that he wasn't going to push me any harder on this. So, after a few minutes, I said, "You wanted to talk about guns?"

He looked at me approvingly, shook his head and chuckled. "You really are a glutton for punishment, aren't you?"

"I guess I'm having a moment of weakness. I'd take advantage of it, if I were you."

"You're sure? This one isn't going to be easy."

I laughed. "Like everything up to this point has been a piece of cake?"

He smiled. "OK." He took a few more steps in silence. "Let's do another short history lesson. This time, contemporary Ireland. I'm sure you know about the conflict in Northern Ireland that lasted from the 60s to the late 90s."

"Of course."

"Did you know that some people identify the deaths of three children in an incident there as a critical event in ending the conflict? Their deaths produced a mass movement for peace, and two women who started it received the Nobel Peace Prize. Granted, the children died in 1976, and it took years before the fighting stopped. But there seems to have been a sense in some quarters—especially among mothers—that things had gone too far."

"Right. I recall something about that now."

"Three children. Thousands of people responded to the deaths of only *three* children." He took a few more steps. "Have you ever been to western Connecticut, Congressman?"

I suspected this is where he'd go, but I honestly didn't

want to discuss this. "No. It's out of my district."

He glowered at me for trying to be glib and evasive. Clearly, this was a more sensitive topic with him than I'd anticipated.

"I lived there for a year. It's a beautiful part of the country. It's as bucolic and peaceful as anyone could want. It's the last place you'd expect 20 children to be gunned down in their elementary school."

I remembered how stunned—and terrified—I was when I heard about the shooting. I knew it was blind paranoia, but I immediately grabbed my phone and called my kids. I needed to know they were safe.

"Look, there's no denying this was a terrible tragedy. The shooter had serious mental problems. But the guns belonged to his mother, right?"

Abe grimaced. "Strictly speaking, yes. They were part of an arsenal her son had access to. But you're splitting hairs. In response to this 'terrible tragedy,' what did Congress do? In particular, tell me what action was taken by all of you who believe the right to life is sacred and who have sworn to defend innocent human life."

"If you just let me ex—"

"Don't even try to dance your way out of this. You did nothing. *Nothing!* Even though 85% of Americans— members of both parties, including gun owners—agree that background checks should be improved. Even though nearly 80% think that people with mental illness shouldn't be able to buy guns. You did nothing! *Three* Irish children die, and it's a huge deal there. *Twenty* American kids get massacred, and the Faux-G.O.P. yawns. Wait! I apologize. You *did* do a few things. The day after terrorists killed 14 people in San Bernadino, you voted down a proposal calling for expanded background checks. Next, you continued to let people on the terrorist watch list get guns. Then you blocked an attempt to stop people with mental illnesses from doing so. And then, when some madman kills 59 people and wounds 489 in Las Vegas you screw up your courage and once again do *nothing*! Wow! Those are real 'Profiles in Courage' moments. You stood up and faced down all those fanatics who wanted to find some way to keep their kids, friends, and neighbors from being massacred. You showed them. Well done, you!"

I groaned at the oversimplification. "I understand where you're coming from, but it's more complicated than that."

He thumped me on the arm—hard. This wasn't a typical 'guy love tap.' He threw that punch with real venom.

"Have you ever noticed how the stuff your crowd *wants* to do is 'clear, simple, and makes common sense,' while anything you *don't* want to do is 'complicated'?

Complicated? Tell me what's so complicated about keeping guns out of the hands of people on the terrorist watch list or those afflicted with mental illness. Let me guess. The bills were too restrictive. Some innocent people may be affected. They may get inconvenienced or have to wait to prove they're entitled to that AK-47 they need to blow away Bambi. And that's *so* much more important than preventing a six-year old from being slaughtered."

He stopped and faced me. "Be straight with me, Congressman. Which is it? Are you a hypocrite or a coward? 'Protecting innocent lives' is important to you when you talk about abortion, but it vanishes when we want to protect school kids? Or do you just lack the balls to do what you know in your heart is right?"

He stared into the distance for a while. He stood rock still and silent. Then he took a deep breath and relaxed. "Let me put it as simply as I can, Congressman. When the next mass killing takes place, think of all those proposals you voted down that might have prevented it. Then see how your finger is one of the ones on the trigger of that gun you let get purchased.

"Your wife gave you that watch for a reason. She was right. Your job is to look after everyone's children. How well are you doing that?" He turned and continued walking.

His last comment rattled me. My position on abortion

is all about preventing the end of an innocent life. But I've always been able to distance myself from my votes on gun rights and the mass shootings. Something about the passion and intensity of Abe's harangue made me feel as though he was accusing me of being complicit in the death of a child he knew—a child he was telling me it had been my job to protect. I needed a few minutes to shake the feeling. I struggled with how to respond.

"And then there's that right-wing militia you're arming," he added glibly, "I suppose nothing says 'America' to the Faux-G.O.P. like a private army willing to lock and load, eh?"

I'd been sure he was ready to move on to another topic. But he was just winding up for another swing. I wasn't going to be dragged into a morass.

"Gun rights are protected by the Second Amendment," I said firmly. "The Supreme Court made that clear."

He stopped and looked at me thoughtfully. "When you were CEO, Congressman, you had a reputation for being a 'details guy.' You read everything related to whatever decision you were mulling over. And you wouldn't settle for the summaries your underlings prepared for you. You looked at the original data. And then you made sure you understood the precise consequences of your decisions. You never wanted to be caught from behind by something you didn't anticipate.

Those are terrific traits."

Abe didn't do gratuitous flattery. He was teeing me up.

He saw my hesitation for what it was. "And your silence says you're suspicious. *Not* such a terrific trait."

I laughed. "Given our exchanges so far, surely you aren't surprised."

"Considering the crowd you've been hanging out with, not at all. What puzzles me is how you could have changed so much. You've traded in facts for propaganda."

"Propaganda? Didn't you already ream me out about truth and facts? You can't go back there. We moved on."

"Yes, we have. To guns. And I'm not talking about lies—but laziness. If you can say the Supreme Court ratified the NRA's position, you haven't read the decision. A *five to four* decision by a court dominated by conservatives. Hardly unanimity. Even then, the decision leaves plenty of room for limiting military-grade hardware like automatic weapons and 100-cartridge ammo clips. If, however, your party is so keen on letting people buy that stuff, the most logical explanation is that you like the idea of vigilante cowboys who will menace your opponents."

"Private militia? Bands of vigilantes? You have a great imagination. You should write fiction."

"Fiction? You're going to dismiss domestic terrorism as a product of my imagination?"

Abe had reverted to exaggerating again. I groaned inside.

"Dismiss terrorism? Hardly. In fact, my concern about terrorism is one of the reasons I back gun rights."

"The reality of the situation, however, is that fear of terrorists is one of the most important reasons to *tighten* controls on guns."

"How does that make any sense?"

Once again, his expression conveyed serious disappointment. He took a deep breath.

"Tell me, Congressman, what's the *second* most deadly terrorist attack in the U.S.?"

"You mean after 9/11?"

"Yes."

"That would have to be the nightclub in Orlando."

"No."

"Are you sure?"

"Positive."

"Then San Bernadino. But I was positive fewer people died there than in Orlando."

"And you were right. But the second worst terrorist attack isn't San Bernadino. Try again. Take your time."

I closed my eyes and tried to recall terrorist incidents. "Sorry, I can't remember anything worse."

"That's because, like most of your crowd, you're ignoring good old fashioned, red, white and blue terrorism. It was the Oklahoma City bombing. One hundred sixty-eight people died, including 19 children, and more than 600 people were injured. Domestic terrorism brought to you by ... not Muslims, Iranians, Egyptians, Syrians, Palestinians, or any of the other groups your gang likes to demonize. It was carried out by two *white right-wing Americans* who were upset at how the FBI handled the Waco siege and Ruby Ridge. Their idea was to spark a revolution against the federal government.

"And that's not the only example of right-wing violence. Since the 1980s, there have been repeated attacks from the right. When you include the abortion violence I mentioned earlier, the body count grows even more. During that same period, the only example of left-wing violence was that terrible ballfield shooting in D.C.

"So, intentionally or not, your defense of 'gun rights' helped arm radical right-wing domestic terrorists. Do you honestly think those assault rifles, automatic weapons, body armor, flamethrowers, cannons, 'mini-guns' that fire up to 6,000 rounds a minute that *you've* made legal are bought by 'hobbyists' who would *never* use them against the people they believe are their enemies? There are near—"

"Wait!" I was shocked. "You're kidding? *Cannons? Flamethrowers?* Everything you mentioned is legal to buy?"

"Yes. Thanks to you and your 'life protecting' cronies.

106

Oh, I forgot the grenade launchers, but—"

"Stop! Grenade launchers? Legal?" I sputtered.

"In fairness, there are hoops to jump through, and getting good ammo is tough. However, …." He smiled wryly. He was going to twist the knife again. "… we can rest comfortably at night knowing that anyone toying with insurrection or terrorism will scrupulously obey the relevant laws. Right?"

I could tell he'd worked up another head of steam. I knew better than interrupt him.

"And I suppose you *also* don't know that there are nearly 1,000 active anti-government groups. More than 250 are militias. We had a huge increase right after Barack Obama was elected President. Surprise, surprise. You're not stupid. You've heard reference to 'Second Amendment solutions'—from Bozo the Clown, no less. You're telling me that crowd wouldn't seriously consider assassinations?"

The idea that we might see political assassinations in the U.S. again shook me to the core.

He looked at me grimly. "Let me ask you again— when did you stop *reading* the laws you vote on? And when did you stop worrying about the consequences of your decisions? When did you become a toady, just taking orders from a bunch of radicals?"

I was so stunned I was still having a hard time

processing this. *Body armor? Flamethrowers? Cannons? Grenade launchers? Legal by my votes?*

Abe studied my face and shook his head in astonishment. "Son of a bitch! You really are surprised. Once again, not even seeing the fire roaring towards you. I owe you an apology. You aren't a coward or a hypocrite. You're stupid!"

He jumped up onto the nearest bench and cupped his hands to his mouth. "Ladies and Gentlemen! Boys and Girls! Children of All Ages! You aren't going to believe this. My friend here, Congressman We-Have-To-Do-Everything-We-Can-To-Protect-the-Sanctity-of-Life has armed a right-wing militia without even knowing it! So, take hope! If someone this clueless and irresponsible can make it to Congress, you can too!"

The scene was so bizarre the few people walking by laughed. My only consolation was that the look on their faces said they thought it was part of an impromptu two-man comedy sketch.

Abe hopped down and looked at me. "Three hundred million guns and assorted weaponry. Lots of those are owned by people who think the government is their enemy. I hope you feel proud."

My head was swimming. I didn't know what to say.

As he turned and started walking again, he clapped me on the back. "Protect innocent life, my ass! You're a real piece of work. On the one hand, my group sees you as someone who demonstrated great skill and intelligence when you were CEO. Our hope was that you'd find your true self and be able to work with us to help the country. But now? Let's see. You're ignorant of key details about the gun issue or you get them wrong."

He stopped walking and turned to me. He took a deep breath and put his hand on my shoulder. "How many times do I have to say this, Stephen?" he asked calmly. "You are head and shoulders better than the bozos who've gotten you to turn off your brain. You are smarter, more caring, more patriotic, and more compassionate. You know how it important it is to make the future better for our children. You wear that watch for a reason. You're fundamentally a good guy. Let me help you get out from under the thumb of those sick bastards telling you what to do."

He pointed to a monument ahead of us. "We're here. The perfect place to start discussing our next topic."

CHAPTER FIVE

Stepping into the World War Two Memorial was like entering a church. Everyone there was either silent, or, if they spoke, they whispered. Abe turned to me and said softly, "I always spend a few minutes here when I visit D.C. Then we'll go somewhere to talk."

I appreciated the opportunity to get centered again. I felt blindsided by what Abe had just told me about guns. How could I not know this? I felt stupid. Abe was right. When I was CEO, there wasn't a detail of a deal or of a part of our operation I wasn't familiar with. When had I stopped paying attention?

And the longer we talked, the more I saw that much of his passion was driven by his *genuine* concern for me. I realized that underlying everything he said in the various topics we'd covered was *disappointment* that I hadn't done better. He wasn't angry—accusing me of being thoughtless, meanspirited, or an ideologue. He was charging me with not doing my best. Not being my own man. Not delivering on my potential. Letting people I knew weren't as smart or as principled tell me what to do.

Walking around the perimeter of the monument let me relax. I took in the grandeur of the spot, and let its meaning soak in. I looked for Abe and saw him stop in front of the Wall of Stars. He stood at attention and snapped a salute. I eventually made my way over there. He was still in the same position. We simply nodded at each other and headed out of the Memorial and sat down on a bench opposite it. Abe was somber—even more so than at the end of our last exchange. I wanted to ask him about the salute, but it felt like prying.

"Do you know how many people died during World War Two, Congressman?"

"It has to be in the millions. I've never heard the exact number. But I'm sure it's staggering."

"Staggering, indeed. When you combine military and civilian deaths, it amounts to more than 60 million— about 4% of the world's population at the time. This monument is for the 400,000 American troops who died. And we aren't even talking about injuries or the social and economic devastation the war caused … All because a bunch of white nationalists in Germany felt they were being pushed around and decided to push back. They wanted to put Germany first … to make Germany great again … to get rid of all those dangerous foreigners… to intimidate opponents … to discredit the press by calling it *lügenpresse*—'fake news.'" He looked at me and raised an eyebrow. "You know the type."

I had a sense from how his mood changed that there was something personal in the mix. I wanted to be respectful, but I didn't agree with where he was taking us. "Don't you think you're blowing things out of proportion?"

"Very possibly."

Given how relentless he'd been on everything else we'd talked about, I was surprised he backed off so quickly.

"In fact, I hope I'm dead wrong," he continued. "But Weimar Germany was the most highly educated country on the planet at the time. I'm sure people there said, 'It can't happen here.' Yet it did. Who was it who said, 'the price of liberty is eternal vigilance'? Am I being vigilant or paranoid? Only time will tell. But, as you gather, my group sees clear threats to the country, and we're deeply troubled by parallels between the Faux-G.O.P. and the Nazis."

I hoped he was baiting me again. When I looked at him carefully, his grim expression said he wasn't. I was stunned.

"Surely, you're overstating."

"Again, maybe I am—but not for dramatic effect. The

Germans didn't recognize the threat early enough, did they? And we don't have to be talking about another World War and gas chambers. My group's worry is the rise of American fascism. Extreme nationalism, authoritarianism, intolerance, racism, suppression of any opposition so lies can't be challenged. The G.O.P. unwittingly made it easier for that crowd to get some traction. That's when you became the Faux-G.O.P. It's no accident that my group is focusing on values like respect, truth, and life. It's everything any fascist wants to exterminate."

I looked at his face again. This wasn't one of his over-the-top rants aimed to provoke me. And by this point in our conversation—despite Abe's occasional insults and exaggerations—I'd come to respect him enough to think he wouldn't accuse other Americans of trying to destroy the country without what *he*, at least, considered to be relevant evidence.

As I tried to figure out how I wanted to respond, he said, "I understand your silence, Congressman. This is ridiculous, insulting, and scary at the same time. But it's too serious a matter for any side in the debate to be wrong about. Let me walk you through how we see it. If you spot any mistakes, throw a flag on the play. I'm serious."

I nodded and waited as he gathered his thoughts.

"This will make more sense to you as a former CEO

than as a politician. Basically, we're talking about the equivalent of making a profit by cobbling together a bunch of niche markets.

"The German Workers Party, which Hitler renamed the National Socialist Party, wasn't all that significant at first. But they appealed to various 'markets' with different parts of their main ideas: Germany was threatened by both inside and outside forces; it needed to be able to stand on its own, economically and militarily; the Aryans were a superior race; and a strong leader was the answer. The appeal to nationalists, authoritarians, racists, and anti-Semites was obvious. Ordinary working people were brought in by promises of improved pensions and public utilities. Farmers were told they could own the land they farmed. Business people liked the idea of the stability that comes with a strong government and the Nazis' antipathy to trade unions and Communists. Anyone unhappy with how the government was handling things was vulnerable to Hitler's charisma."

"OK," I said seriously. "Where are the parallels?"

"The current Republican party isn't the political party you joined. It's now a patchwork of niche markets which is the result of the party trying to adapt to a changing America over the last few decades. You still have some of your traditional market segments—business, the rich, and college educated whites. But your growth has been in the far Right and the far-far Right. After the Southern Strategy, you added the Christian Right. Next, the Tea Party. Then, the 'gun rights' crowd, anti-abortionists, anti-government groups, the anti-immigration crowd, white nationalists, people who want to deny science, and, more recently, disaffected blue collar workers. You promised something different to each—either through 'code' and 'dog whistles,' or, more recent, explicitly: wealth, jobs, low taxes, banning abortion, gutting the EPA, guns, a weak federal government, deporting anyone not white, sympathy for 'white culture.' And when you put these groups together, you've got enough to win elections. Unfortunately, as you kept tilting to the right, you let everyone from racists and xenophobes to conspiracy nuts imagine you support them. And now the right-wing extremists run the Party."

He paused. "Anything inaccurate so far?"

I shook my head. "Sadly, no."

"So, let's see what the Faux-G.O.P. has given us, and you tell me whether there's any reason to worry about where the country is heading. We start with the narcissist bully who admires dictators and makes things up out of whole cloth. He claims the press is 'the enemy of the American people.' He demonizes honest, hard-working immigrants, while defending child molesters and wife beaters. Everything about him and Russia says he's guilty

116

as sin. He attacks the FBI, the DOJ, and the intelligence community. He wants the very groups designed to protect us to be a personal police force that will go after his enemies. He threatens nuclear war. He tries to rally his following by stoking irrational fears. Intellectually, even his loyalists think he's a moron. He's thoroughly incompetent at his job. Internationally, he's a joke—a *dangerous* joke, but still a joke. He scares our allies and cozies up to our enemies. He surrounds himself with radical right-wing propagandists and provocateurs, doesn't care about anything but his massive ego, his wallet, and keeping himself and his kids out of jail ..."

He waved his hand indicating the never-ending list of troubling traits and actions we both knew, but had no desire to go into more detail about.

"And how has your party responded? For starters, after you called this guy a bozo during the campaign, as soon he was elected, you sucked up to him in the hope you could ram through an extreme agenda. You're denying climate change and weakening protections of clean air and water. You don't hesitate to confirm senior officials for the Administration who are either incompetent, have major conflicts of interest, and then use their office to profit themselves, friends, or family. You're trying your best to deprive millions of Americans of their health insurance and deport hundreds of thousands of people whose real crime is that they aren't white. You want to set Wall Street loose against us again. And despite decades of being a bunch of 'deficit scolds,' you've now decided that an additional $1 trillion is inconsequential."

He stopped for a moment and looked at me—again with a look of deep worry. "What do we call this, Congressman? Seeing the fire and not warning anyone? No. Not seeing the fire? No. Something much worse— throwing more wood on the fire as it approaches us!"

All of this hit so close to some private worries I'd never voiced, I had no enthusiasm to object.

"Let me make this easier for you, Congressman. Forget the historical parallels, and imagine what a neutral observer would conclude from the Faux-Republican 'hit parade' over the last 20 years: extremist legislation and executive orders that don't reflect the perspective of most Americans; your party's repeated willingness to shut down the government; holding the country's credit rating hostage; gerrymandering like crazy to have white districts; favoring the rich so much that we have historic and frightening concentrations of wealth and power; screwing the lower and middle class; an ongoing war against women; your resistance to work with our first Black President on *anything*, and your rabid characterization of him as some sort of enemy; a 'my way or no way' attitude about everything; stealing the Supreme Court nomination. You want to reduce government spending on everything except weapons—even if it's on the infrastructure business needs to succeed. You oppose health care reform—even when the pre-existing condition restriction could bankrupt families. You can't wait to eradicate Dodd-Frank—even though it increases the risks of another disaster. It's more important to advance the Republican theology than to do some practical good for the citizenry.

You look at elections like a sporting event where it's 'winner take all.' You apparently forget that when you take the oath of office as a Congressman, you swear to support the Constitution, not to divide the spoils. Is that what *keeping a promise* means to your party?"

"I wondered when we were going to get to that."

"So," he looked at me approvingly, "it's been on your mind. Good. I got the feeling promises matter to you. You see yourself as a stand-up guy. Remind me, then, what you all promise in the oath."

That was easy. I had a framed copy on my office wall and read it regularly. The problem was that over the last few years, doing so made me increasingly uncomfortable.

"We swear to support and defend the Constitution against all enemies, foreign and domestic, and bear true faith and allegiance."

He nodded. "I'm impressed. I wonder how many of your colleagues can do that without choking on it. But you're troubled because, in your heart, you're a patriotic idealist. You don't think 'bearing true faith and allegiance' describes what your party has been doing. And since you're realistic, you know what the party's big accomplishments actually have been. Military adventurism. Economic devastation because of your belief in the evils of regulation. A historic concentration of wealth. Denial of the biggest danger facing the planet. A radically conservative Supreme Court. And you paved the way for the greatest threat to American democracy in my lifetime."

He had such momentum, I was surprised he stopped.

"Very interesting." He looked at me and raised an eyebrow. "I hit a raw nerve, didn't I? Whether you know it or not, you winced when I said, *threat to democracy*. Care to explain that worried look?"

"You're perceptive. I'm impressed. I read something very disturbing in *The Economist* recently. They do an annual 'Democracy Index,' and I'm embarrassed to say I'd never noticed it before. I must have breezed right past it."

"So, why did it catch your eye this year?"

"Because it was nothing but seriously bad news. First, democracy is losing ground. In 2015, 8.9 percent of the world's population lived in fully functioning democracies. In 2017, it dropped to only 4.5 percent."

"You're right. That is bad news."

"But the worst part is it dropped because the U.S. was downgraded from a 'full' democracy to a 'flawed' democracy."

"Thanks to—"

I swallowed hard. "Thanks to my party."

"I appreciate your honesty, Stephen, and how difficult it is to admit this. But given the coup the G.O.P. pulled off, you can't be surprised, can you? I mean, you can be *disappointed*, but not *surprised*."

I did a double-take. "Wait! Did you say *coup*?" I thought we'd gotten to a place where Abe wasn't doing overstatement and exaggeration any more. Had he gone back to trying to provoke me? His face said, 'no.'

"We engineered a coup somewhere that overturned a democracy? Seriously?" I wracked my brain trying to recall any military takeovers in the last decade. "Egypt? Thailand? Yemen? Venezuela? It's inconceivable to me that the Republican Party had anything to do with any of them."

"You're right. It didn't. Think closer to home."

I tried again and came up empty. "You're going to have to give me a hint."

"Fine," he nodded. He swept his hand in a circle over his head, pointing in every direction. "Capitol Hill. Washington Monument. Arlington National Cemetery."

I was confused. Abe seemed deadly serious. But this was crazy. "What do you mean? There has *not* been a military coup in the United States."

He looked at me somberly. "Did I say *military* coup, Stephen?"

The earnestness in his voice was unsettling. He meant it. A Republican *coup*?

"So what other kind is there?'"

"I consider *any* illegitimate seizure of power to be a *coup*."

"The G.O.P. has seized power—illegitimately."

"Yes."

I shook my head in disbelief. I looked at him again. He was serious. "How?"

"Coups can be accomplished in a variety of ways. Tanks in the street. Disbanding a democratically elected legislature. Using legitimate laws to game the system for the sake of taking over."

"So, since Congress still exists, and there was no military takeover, you must be talking about the last one."

"Correct."

"So, this *coup* was *legal*."

"In one sense, yes."

"Let me get this straight. There's been a coup. But our key governmental institutions are in place. And no laws have been broken."

"You weren't listening. I said the coup was legal 'in one sense.' You're taking too narrow a view. Just because actions are legal doesn't make them legitimate. My definition of a coup was an *illegitimate* seizure of power."

"You're saying, then, that whatever *legal* actions that were part of the coup weren't *legitimate.*"

"Correct."

"But if that's the case, wouldn't' those actions and those laws be challenged in the courts and in legislatures?"

"Yes. And in some cases, they are. But not enough people noticed the coup when it was planned and put into place to stop it. In fact, most people still don't know it happened. If they did, I can promise you they'd be in the streets over this. That's why my group decided to take action. We aren't going to tolerate an attack on democracy that has been pulled off by undermining all the key ethical values we've been talking about." The rising anger in his voice surprised me, but only reinforced his sincerity.

I was still confused. "You have to believe me when I say I'm not being obstreperous. But I'm having trouble grasping the idea that a genuine *coup d'etat*—an illegitimate seizure of power—has been carried out by the Republican Party. A coup that has struck at the very heart of democracy, was *legal*, but millions of Americans haven't noticed. Not even the Democrats. Nor the British. Nor the French. Nor any other democratic nation. All of whom would surely would issue a call to arms in defense of democracy."

"Yes. I'd expect they would, if they noticed."

"Doesn't that sound simply unbelievable?"

"Not just unbelievable. It's frightening, shocking, and depressing that the Faux-G.O.P. was able to pull it off. They're a bunch of miserable, disloyal, unpatriotic, little shits." He punctuated each epithet by angrily poking his finger in the air. "But you've got to admire what such a group of worthless, authoritarian, proto-fascists did."

I couldn't help but laugh. "You know, Abe, you need to get over being so reticent. Tell me what you really think."

Even he had to laugh at himself.

"But if there's been a coup, what's your evidence?"

He chuckled. "It took you long enough to ask. The evidence is in how you were able to impose minority rule in the country."

Again, I was puzzled. "We don't have minority rule. There may have been meddling in the 2016 election, but there's virtually no evidence of voter fraud. Our elections are basically fair."

"Then how do you explain the fact that most of the policies and goals the G.O.P. champions don't reflect the will of the majority? Isn't that supposed to be what democracy is all about? The will of the majority?"

"Right—which is what we have."

He shook his head. "That's what we *say* we have. But we *don't*. Here's why. Think about what the G.O.P. stands for. Your party is rabidly anti-abortion, denies climate change, demonizes anyone who isn't a white heterosexual, and passes tax legislation that benefits wealthy individuals and corporations. You can't stop trying to repeal Obamacare.

"*However*, the majority of Americans opposes all that. Repealing Obamacare is supported by less than a third of the population. Sixty percent think that abortion should be legal. That's even higher—65%—for Americans under 30. Sixty-two percent support same-sex marriage. Less than a third think that the current distribution of wealth is 'fair.' And only 25% liked your tax plan. On his best day, that racist you gave us has an approval rating of, what, 35%? Yet most Republicans in Congress do nothing while he pisses on any number of norms and institutions we *all* know are critical to the good of the country—no matter who's in power.

Like I said, *minority rule*. ... Tell me what you think this is."

He pulled out his tablet again and showed me a strange image.

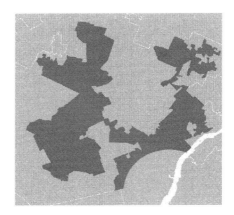

I could tell he had fallen back into 'setting me up' mode. "Is this a Rorschach test?

"Something like that. Humor me."

I laughed. "Two people dancing?"

"Very good! Actually, two *Republicans* dancing because they've been able to gerrymander like crazy to stack the deck. This is the Pennsylvania 7th Congressional District. Just one of many we could look at. You know as well as I do which factors get districts drawn this way. The federal court in Richmond found that the primary purpose of North Carolina's gerrymandering wasn't to stop voter fraud, but rather to disenfranchise minority voters. And it wasn't even subtle. The justices said African Americans were targeted 'with almost surgical precision.' Now when you do this sort of thing on a statewide basis, you've able to make Republican votes count more than Democratic votes. For example, the gerrymandering in Wisconsin let Republicans win 60% of the seats in the State Assembly with only 48.6% of the votes. The Democrats would have to win more than 53% of the votes to win a majority of seats. In my opinion, the G.O.P.'s REDMAP project might just as well have been called, The Plot to Overthrow Democracy."

I prided myself in having a sense of fair play. I wasn't the kind of person who thought, "If you aren't cheating, you aren't trying." My feeling was, "If you cheat, it's because you know you can't win." Some of my colleagues were crowing at the success of REDMAP, but not me. When you put it together with everything going on now, the way my party acted wasn't just unfair, it was—

"You aren't pushing back, Congressman." He interrupted my rumination. "I'm pleased. I've been relying on your reputation as a facts/data/evidence guy. I was confident that by the time we got to this part of our conversation, we'd agree more than disagree." He looked at me sympathetically. "But I get the feeling you're troubled about more than mere promise breaking and cheating."

I nodded. "OK, but now you humor me. Let's see how well you know me. You tell me what's bothering me."

"Easy. If you're worried about the way your party is threatening democracy, there's the 'Russia connection.'

Your guy publicly praises a vicious autocrat who has probably ordered the assassination of critics and who tries to undermine democracies. He invaded Ukraine. He's meddled in Europe's elections. He tried to influence *our* election. He engaged in *cyber-warfare*. This was an *attack* on Americans.

"Yet your guy downplays any threat from Russia. Hell, even though virtually every security agency has concluded the Russians attacked us, Comrade Pinocchio dismisses it as a hoax! He refused to implement appropriate sanctions. What message do you suppose that sends to the Kremlin? What part of 'preserve, protect and defend the Constitution' doesn't he understand? Christ! Giving the Russians sensitive intelligence! Refusing to take action! If that doesn't represent a major threat to American democracy, what does? And what do the toadies in your party do? They give him cover!" He looked at me grimly. "How'd I do?"

I took a deep breath. This was the first time I was going to say this out loud. "There's a time where patriotism is more important than party loyalty—when everyone has to choose a side. I've been increasingly worried that we're there now and that people in my party are choosing the wrong side.

"I believe that a key part of American democracy is separation of powers, our system of checks and balances, and a legal system that's not politicized. I find this war against the FBI, the DOJ, and the intelligence community—all for nothing more than political gain— deeply troubling … short-sighted … suspicious.

"I saw an interesting interview with a former senior official at the FBI. He made a great case about how much damage was probably being done to the thousands of cases the Bureau works on ever day—terrorism, cybercrime, organized crime, human trafficking, and so on. He said, 'I worry about the impact on a jury of saying the FBI's prosecutions are politically motivated. What are they thinking now when they listen to an FBI agent testifying in a public corruption case?' But members of my party don't seem to care about any of that. And a lot of them are *lawyers*—which means they understand the damage being done."

"Good point. Troubling. But *suspicious?*"

"On the heels of 9/11, there was no doubt that we had to investigate what happened and find ways to prevent something like that from happening again. When the Russia meddling in the election was first explained to us in Congress, we were stunned. Our primary global adversary interfered with our election. Some Americans may even have helped them. As with 9/11, everyone was on board. Then, slowly, things changed. Some of my colleagues simply dragged their feet. But others began working as hard as they could to derail the investigation.

"Now if this were a different kind of issue, I could dismiss that as party politics. But this was an attack by a foreign enemy. Why would you want to kill that kind of investigation?"

"Excellent question. Your answer?"

"I can think of only three reasons. First, mind numbing, self-interested party loyalty."

Abe laughed. "Well, there's no shortage of that on both sides of the aisle. Second reason?"

"You colluded with the attack because you believe the ends justify the means, and there's evidence somewhere that proves it."

"You're trying to protect yourself."

"Right. Stupid and selfish, I get. But *suspicious*? That must be your third reason."

I sat quietly for a moment before I could say the words. "This is the one I can't believe I'm saying out loud. You're a Member of the United States Congress who wants to see our democracy destroyed and replaced with authoritarianism. You have a stronger allegiance to our enemies than to democracy and to America. You want to stop the rest of us from protecting ourselves from subsequent attacks."

Abe sat still for a few seconds and took a deep breath. "Treason," he said grimly.

I paused and asked myself if I really meant that. I nodded my head. "Yes."

Abe shook his head sadly. "My group came to the same conclusion. We use a simple, values-based definition of treason—not the legalistic 'waging war against the country' or 'giving aid and comfort' to our enemies. To us, treason is simply 'Violating your allegiance to your country.' We think that 'allegiance to America' means aggressively pursuing anyone—foreign or domestic— who wants to harm it by undermining its core institutions. We take a very hard line on this. It's not just people who collude with the enemy. We think that anyone who obstructs the attempt to protect ourselves or injects politics into the process to muddy the waters is falling short on their allegiance to the country. In our book, that's treason."

He pointed to the monument. "Do you think the 400,000 men and women this place honors would be pleased to know *that's* what they died for? This is a great country. We used to have a sense of common purpose. But we've been at each other's throats for at least the last couple of decades. Politics used to be conducted with civility. Public servants actually tried to accomplish something. Now it's a blood sport. We used to be the country everyone else wanted to be. And now? Millions of people *around the world* marched in protest the day after your guy's inauguration. Our allies don't know if we're dependable. Our enemies are already trying to capitalize on the chaos, and members of your party aren't up in arms trying to stop them. I am no longer certain of the character of my own country and of my fellow citizens. And what I fear fills me with dread."

Abe's voice overflowed with anger and sadness. This wasn't anything like his earlier rants which, it was clear to me now, were designed to provoke me. He wasn't accusing. He was ticking off a massively depressing catalogue of threats both he and I believed were true.

CHAPTER SIX

Abe abruptly stood up. "Come on. I think a change of scene would help."

We walked along the side of the reflecting pool for a few minutes.

"I'm surprised you haven't asked me what kind of work I do."

I was jarred by the abrupt change of topic.

"What did you say?"

"Sorry. Sometimes I find all this so depressing, I have to think about something else for a while."

"OK. I assume you're a professional political operative. You're the public face of the 'group' you keep referring to."

"Nope. I run a specialty consulting firm that specializes in preventing corporate disasters. We get called when a company uncovers the early stage of a major problem and wants to make sure things don't blow up. My talent is identifying 'worst case scenarios' and knowing what has to be done to defuse them. In fact, what first brought you to my attention was the way you kept your company from crashing. That was a very nice piece of work."

"Thanks," I said. "One of the things I'm most proud of is my ability to see patterns in data. I don't know why I'm so good at it, but I am. That's why I could turn the company around. We were against the wall, we knew we had only one shot, and we were considering a few new products. There were some small, but critical details in the market analysis that made me choose the one we went with. I could see a trend—momentum—that no one else could. When we were so successful, everyone thought I was a genius. I wasn't. I was just sensitive to what the data said."

He pulled a piece of paper out of his pocket, unfolded it and handed it to me. "I thought you'd be interested to know how you first came to my attention."

It was an old article from the *Wall Street Journal*, "Radical Idea Makes Radical Profits." The story was about how I turned the company around after being named CEO.

"Interesting strategy," he observed. "Telling everyone that for the next six months, no one could talk about anything to do with money—profits, costs—at any meeting. There would be only one focus—making the *best products*, delivering the *best service* to customers and doing it in the *most supportive working conditions* possible. I'm surprised your Board didn't yank you as soon as they got wind of this."

I laughed. "In fact, some members wanted to. But when I agreed to be CEO, I made sure the Board couldn't touch me for at least a year. I even gave up some compensation to get that in the agreement. Now they realized why. In the end, it didn't matter because of how successful the strategy was. Within the year, we had explosive growth on every front."

"It was a gutsy move." He nodded approval. "But since your company was two clicks from closing down, I suppose a 'Hail Mary' play was about all you could try."

"Act of desperation? No. I was positive everything would work out as it did."

"I had a feeling that was the case," he smiled. "But in the *Journal* article, all you say is, 'Approaching business this way just makes sense.' I felt sure there was more to it than that. What's the real story?"

When I looked at him, I saw genuine interest and respect. I was glad to see this seemed like another area we'd agree about.

"When I was in business school, I'm embarrassed to

say that I slept through one of those required 'business and society' courses—*except* for the day we had a guest speaker. Like you, he was an odd duck. A venture capitalist friend of the professor who introduced himself only as 'Socrates.' He reached into his jacket, took out a wad of bills and put them on the table. 'That's $5,000— 50 hundreds. I wager that no one in this room believes that the main point of a business is to make money.' Everybody chuckled at how ridiculous it was to say that at a business school. We were all eyeing the cash and just waiting to see how we could get it. 'But in my world,' he continued, 'reward requires risk. So, if you want a shot at the prize, you have to risk ... how much? You're all students. Let's say twenty dollars.' The prospect of such easy money had us on the edges of our seats. 'Who's in?' Every hand shot up. He turned to the professor with a chuckle, 'What have you been teaching these people, Jane? Or are they just too cocky for their own good?' She looked at the 50 faces salivating over the green bills then gave Socrates a look I didn't understand at the time. Now I realize it said, 'It's going to be like shooting fish in a barrel. Go ahead. They asked for it.'

"Then he continued. 'Since everyone's in, we'll work on this as a group. If even one person isn't convinced of my point of view, everyone will get a hundred. That's a five-fold return on your 20. Seem fair?" Everyone scrambled for their wallets and anteed up before he could change his mind.

"When the smoke cleared at the end of class, he swept all the money on the table into his briefcase with a self-satisfied grin. 'Lest you think I've taken advantage of you,' he explained, 'your money will be added to mine and donated to a women's shelter I support. We thank you for your generosity.'

"The argument he used to beat us was so powerful, I never forgot it. When I was named CEO, I decided to try his ideas in real life. It made such common sense, I was sure it would work."

Abe had been listening intensely. "And the secret to his—and your—success?"

"Two surprisingly simple ideas. For the first one, he started by asking who was a fan of Milton Friedman's *Capitalism and Freedom*—a book we'd read earlier in the term. Not surprisingly, everyone's hand went up. Then he did a lot of asking questions and getting answers from different people in the class about why. He cleverly steered us to where we all agreed that the core strength of capitalism is the way it protects *freedom*—through the free market, voluntary transactions and the like.

"Then he asked us to imagine a contract we were asked to sign agreeing to the proposition that the primary object in any business we'd deal with was to make money.

At first, most of us said we would. But when his 'Socratic questioning,' as he called it, showed that we'd want to add conditions—for example, there was no fraud or manipulation, products would have to be safe and as represented, services would be reasonable quality—it was clear no one would *freely agree* to a blanket 'business is mainly about making money.' Everyone agreed that maximizing profits was OK *as long as* we got whatever led us to do business with some individual or company in the first place—something that we needed or wanted. But we all felt that the risks were too high to agree that profits could override everything."

"Clever fellow. But you said he used *two* simple ideas."

"Right. It was bad enough he'd bested the entire room. But then he pulled something you would have loved. In fact, the two of you are annoyingly similar," I joked.

He responded with a big smile.

"He offered us a second chance. Same claim—the main point of a business is to make money. He'd even double the odds. The buy-in was another $20. Everyone looked around. We were sure we could take him because now we were wise to how he operated. The pile of bills on the table grew.

This time, he asked us to imagine that we lived in a small village. How did the inhabitants organize work so that everyone got what they needed?"

"Let me guess." Abe thought for a bit. "Division of labor and specialization of labor? Because it's efficient."

"Exactly. Then he asked the same thing about a bigger community."

"Same answer."

"Correct. Except we're talking about big segments of society, each one organized around a specific goal or function which tells us, as he put it, what its 'job' in the community is. For example, the 'job of education' is to provide people with the skills needed to operate successfully in the society. The 'job of medical operations' is health. The 'job of government' is ensuring social order and doing any key thing we need that other institutions are missing. The 'job' of every segment of society was to give the inhabitants something they wanted or needed in order to live a decent life."

"Got it. So, what does the 'job of business' turn out to be?"

"That was the edge of the cliff he led us to before he pushed us over. We all agreed it's to provide the material goods and services everyone in the community needs?"

"And *profit*?"

"By the time he was done with us, we couldn't deny that it was just a means to an end. A critically important means. But not the central aim of business. The main point of the business in the village is to support a certain kind of life for the people who live there—and that includes a satisfying work life.

"So that's what I told our employees to focus on. We would give our *customers* something they wanted. We'd give our *employees* a place they were happy to go do each day."

"Wait. You used the idea that profits aren't the point of business to turn your company around? Nervy. Very impressive. But counterintuitive."

"Yes and no. What struck me was the way Socrates kept getting us to think about business on a very small scale—like the shoemaker in a village. He's not just—or mainly—the guy you buy shoes from. He's your neighbor. You want him to be successful and make good shoes for everyone. He wants you to be happy. Both of you want each other to care about one another's wants and needs. It's the same with all the other businesses in the village. They provide what everyone needs and wants for a comfortable life. And in that situation, there should be mutual loyalty and support. It made me positive that if we could get our employees and customers alike to see that our *primary* aim was to support a certain high quality of life, we couldn't fail. The most talented people would want to work for us. Customers would not only get great products and services, they'd feel good about supporting such a company.

"So, the day after I was named CEO, I told people to think of us as living in that small village. Focus on giving customers what they want in a way that makes them feel seen, heard and respected. I told managers to treat employees as neighbors in their own community. Positive relationships among all the players were critical. Our mantra became, 'the job of business is to produce a good life for as many people in the village as possible.' I told everyone to think about us as a *service* business."

Abe clapped me on the back. "I knew I was right about you, Stephen."

I was stunned at something so out-of-character. When I looked at him, he was smiling.

I laughed. "So, do you want to tell me why you've gone all 'warm and fuzzy' all of a sudden?"

"The next value we were going to discuss. You're already there. *Service*. So, keep going. That's your idea of *business*. And if I remember correctly, in every one of your campaigns, you've argued that government should 'run like a business.' Given your view of business, I'm intrigued to hear what that means."

"It's not an exact translation—and we can set aside the international dimension—but, from a domestic standpoint, the basics are pretty straightforward. After all, one of the main insights I took away from Socrates is that the reason we organize society as we do is to provide a decent life for the people who live in it. The job of government, then, is service.

"Government isn't some evil entity you fear or go to war with. It's your neighbors. It does what business can't, won't or shouldn't do. A safety net or backstop for all of us when times get hard. Protection of everybody's rights. Defense. Big infrastructure projects. Bridges. Dams. Highways. The electric grid. Public utilities. A safe environment in which to live—now and for our children and grandchildren.

"Also, like a company, you want *everyone* to want to do business with you. So, we don't want any of these 'culture wars' that alienate potential customers. When you run government like a business, you treat everyone with proper respect. Your job is to *do* things to make the country better. In a democracy, that means doing things for your bosses—the citizenry. And you deliver so well on your promises that people are willing to pay a premium."

"OK, but sounds expensive. How do you handle the costs of this upscale operation?"

"Like any other business. You charge according to costs plus what you need to reinvest in the enterprise to keep it healthy. We're a wealthy country. People need to pay their fair share. And those with the most money need to pay up."

"Then you're not a 'starve the beast' guy."